PUB STROLLS IN

DORSET

Anne-Marie Edwards

COUNTRYSIDE BOOKS
NEWBURY BERKSHIRE

First published 2001
© Anne-Marie Edwards 2001
Reprinted 2008

COUNTRYSIDE BOOKS
3 Catherine Road
Newbury, Berkshire

To view our complete range of books,
please visit us at
www.countrysidebooks.co.uk

ISBN 978 1 85306 676 4

Designed by Graham Whiteman

Photographs by Mike Edwards
Maps by Gelder design & mapping

Produced through MRM Associates Ltd., Reading
Printed in Thailand

*All material for the manufacture of this book
was sourced from sustainable forests.*

Contents

INTRODUCTION   6

WALK

1   SYMONDSBURY – The Ilchester Arms ($2^1/_2$ miles)   7

2   MELPLASH – The Half Moon Inn (3 miles)   10

3   NETTLECOMBE – The Marquis of Lorne ($1^1/_2$ or $2^1/_2$ miles)   13

4   CORSCOMBE – The Fox Inn (3 miles)   16

5   EVERSHOT – The Acorn Inn (4 miles)   19

6   THORNFORD – The King's Arms Inn (3 miles)   22

7   PUNCKNOWLE – The Crown Inn ($1^3/_4$ miles)   25

8   ABBOTSBURY – The Ilchester Arms (2 miles)   28

9   LANGTON HERRING – The Elm Tree Inn ($2^1/_2$ miles)   31

10   PORTLAND – The Pulpit Inn (3 miles)   34

11   CHARMINSTER – The Three Compasses (2 miles)   37

12   CERNE ABBAS – The New Inn (3 miles)   40

13   BUCKLAND NEWTON – The Gaggle of Geese (3 miles)   43

14   STOURTON CAUNDLE – The Trooper Inn ($3^1/_2$ miles)   46

15   ANSTY – The Fox Inn ($2^1/_4$ miles)   49

16   WEST KNIGHTON – The New Inn ($2^1/_2$ miles)   52

17   OSMINGTON MILLS – The Smugglers' Inn (3 miles)   55

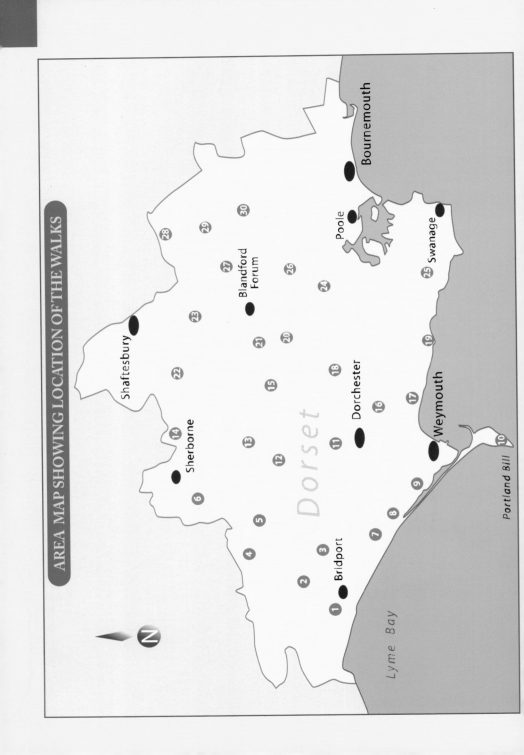

AREA MAP SHOWING LOCATION OF THE WALKS

WALK

18 TOLPUDDLE – The Martyrs' Inn (3 miles)   58

19 LULWORTH COVE – The Lulworth Cove Hotel (1³/₄ miles)   61

20 WINTERBORNE WHITECHURCH – The Milton Arms (3 miles)   64

21 WINTERBORNE STICKLAND – The Shire Horse (3 miles)   67

22 HINTON ST MARY – The White Horse Inn (3 miles)   70

23 IWERNE COURTNEY – The Cricketers (2¹/₂ miles)   73

24 MORDEN – The Cock and Bottle (2 or 3³/₄ miles)   76

25 CHURCH KNOWLE – The New Inn (1³/₄ miles)   79

26 STURMINSTER MARSHALL – The Red Lion Inn (2³/₄ mile)   82

27 TARRANT MONKTON – The Langton Arms (3 miles)   85

28 SIXPENNY HANDLEY – The Roebuck Inn (3 miles)   88

29 GUSSAGE ALL SAINTS – The Drovers' Inn (3 miles)   91

30 HORTON – Drusilla's Inn (2¹/₂ miles)   94

PUBLISHER'S NOTE

We hope that you obtain considerable enjoyment from this book; great care has been taken in its preparation. However, changes of landlord and actual pub closures are sadly not uncommon. Likewise, although at the time of publication all routes followed public rights of way or permitted paths, diversion orders can be made and permissions withdrawn.

We cannot, of course, be held responsible for such diversion orders and any inaccuracies in the text which result from these or any other changes to the routes nor any damage which might result from walkers trespassing on private property. We are anxious though that all details covering the walks and the pubs are kept up to date and would therefore welcome information from readers which would be relevant to future editions.

The sketch maps accompanying each walk are not always to scale and are intended to guide you to the starting point and give a simple but accurate idea of the route to be taken. For those who like the benefit of detailed maps, we recommend that you arm yourself with the relevant Ordnance Survey map in either the Outdoor Leisure or Explorer series.

Dorset is a walker's county. The pace of life is tranquil and unhurried and the country-side is outstandingly beautiful and varied. Turn off the busy roads and you can still find reminders of the landscape Thomas Hardy immortalised in his novels: villages and farms built of golden stone cupped in the downs, magnificent views from inland and coastal hills and lush river valleys rich in wildlife. In early spring the lanes are bordered with snowdrops and in May woods and copses are fragrant with blue-bells. As you walk you will find history round every corner. You can follow in the footsteps of Bronze Age traders along their ridgeway tracks and climb the embank-ments of forts raised around Dorset's hilltops by Iron Age warriors. Medieval farmers have terraced the hillsides with strip lynchets and memories of the Civil War linger in the villages.

We walk in the coastal hills and discover Symondsbury and Puncknowle, old world villages where time seems to have stood still. Further east, the waters of England's largest lagoon, the Fleet, are trapped behind the Chesil Beach. At its western end the historic village of Abbotsbury, well known for its Swannery, provides the setting for an exciting walk from the ruins of the abbey founded here by the Benedictines in the 11th century to the lonely chapel of St Catherine crowning a nearby clifftop. Other coastal walks include a visit to Portland with its mysterious 'lawns' and Church Knowle where you will enjoy splendid views over the Purbeck Hills.

Forming the heart of Dorset is a great range of chalk downland threaded by narrow valleys carved by the county's main rivers and streams. Delightful villages cluster along their banks. We follow riverside paths to explore some of these including Ansty in the shade of Bulbarrow, Nettlecombe tucked away in a valley in the west of the county, and Cerne Abbas famous for its giant.

North of the downs Dorset springs a surprise! Suddenly the chalk escarpment ceases and at its foot lies the Blackmoor Vale, once a great forest, now a green world of small thickly-hedged fields, tiny streams and narrow winding lanes. One of the strolls leads from the village of Hinton St Mary, with its ancient manor house.

The walks in this book may be short – between 1½ and 4 miles – but that is no reason why you should not combine them with a visit to a good pub! All the walks are circular and start at, or close to, a hostelry where you can be sure of a warm welcome and excellent food and drink. The publicans I spoke to were happy to allow patrons to leave cars while they walk but they do ask us to seek their permission first. In cases where this is particularly necessary, or another parking location is used, I have added a note in the appropriate section.

These are real country walks following paths which can often be muddy or slippery so it is wise to wear strong shoes or boots. Finally, I wish you many happy hours exploring this enchanting county. Happy strolling!

Anne-Marie Edwards

Symondsbury

ANCIENT TRACKWAYS IN THE WESTERN HILLS

The Ilchester Arms

MAP: OS EXPLORER 116 (FORMERY 29) (GR 445935)	WALK 1	DISTANCE: 2½ MILES

DIRECTIONS TO START: SYMONDSBURY IS A SMALL WEST DORSET VILLAGE 2 MILES WEST OF BRIDPORT. APPROACHING ALONG THE BRIDPORT BYPASS TURN RIGHT FOLLOWING THE SIGN FOR SYMONDSBURY, DRIVE INTO THE VILLAGE AND THE PUB IS ON YOUR RIGHT. APPROACHING FROM BRIDPORT ALONG THE B3162 TURN RIGHT AT THE SECOND SIGN FOR SYMONDSBURY. APPROACHING FROM THE WEST ALONG THE A35 TURN LEFT FOLLOWING THE FIRST SIGN TO SYMONDSBURY
PARKING: IN THE PUB CAR PARK.

This walk is the perfect introduction to the glorious countryside of West Dorset, a green world of smoothly rounded hills and wooded valleys with villages built of golden sandstone half-hidden among the trees. One of the prettiest of these villages is Symondsbury, tucked in a hollow at the foot of cone-shaped Colmer's Hill, not far from the sea. Thatched cottages and larger Georgian houses cluster around a fine church dating from the 14th century. From the village we take a sunken trackway leading gently uphill to follow a ridge with magnificent views south to the sea and inland to some of Dorset's highest hills. Field paths – alongside blue-flowered flax in summer – lead back to the village.

The Ilchester Arms

A village as charming as Symondsbury deserves an equally attractive pub and the Ilchester Arms fits the picture perfectly. A roof of dark thatch overhangs sturdy walls and stone-mullioned windows. Sometime early in the 14th century the house was built by order of the Abbots of Cerne using what came easily to hand – glowing local stone and hand-hewn solid oak timbers from the shipyards at West Bay. The timbers supporting the roof in the bar were originally intended to form the keels of ships. When the huge inglenook fireplace was discovered behind a modern grate, a scrap of a 160 year old newspaper was also found. It now has pride of place on the wall above.

There is a separate, very comfortable restaurant. Here, or in the bar, you can choose from a wide variety of appetising dishes. Snacks range from ploughman's lunches and omelettes to prawn fritters with Marie Rose sauce, deep fried whitebait and crispy coated Camembert with raspberry sauce. Examples of main meals are plaice stuffed with prawns and mushrooms and lamb moussaka with aubergines and onions cooked in white wine and topped with cheese. Real ales include Palmers Bridport Bitter, IPA and 200.

Opening times are from 11 am to 2.30 pm and 6.30 pm to 11 pm. Food is served from 12 noon to 2 pm and 7 pm to 9 pm. There is a pleasant streamside garden and children's play area. At weekends book your meal beforehand. Telephone: 01308 422600.

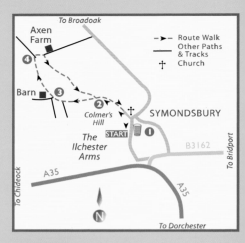

The Walk

① Leave the front porch of the pub and turn right. On the left you pass an imposing Georgian building, the former rectory. When the road curves right keep straight ahead up the no-through-road. The lane passes a row of picturesque cottages and becomes a track leading gradually uphill between high banks hung with ferns and bordered by trees. This ancient pathway is described in Ronald Good's *The Old Roads of Dorset* as 'one of the finest and most impressive old roads in this part of Dorset'.

② The track levels and leads past a joining track on the right which is our return route. Keep to the main track as it curves a little left and then right still between the high sandstone banks. In some places passers-by have carved their initials. An isolated thatched cottage appears on the right – note the beautifully constructed treehouse! Now the banks on either side rise even higher, to around 30 feet, forming an impressive gorge. Just past a track on the left our way curves right to a junction of several paths and a finger post.

The ancient sunken track leading round Colmer's Hill

③ Keep ahead along a grassy path signed for Axen past a barn on your left. You are now following a high ridge with low hedges on either side revealing splendid views. Continue along the ridge for about ¾ mile to a grassy track on the right leading downhill towards a farm.

④ Turn right down the track. After about 150 yards, before you come to the farm, turn right through a gate and down a grassy path which soon rises to run through a gap in a hedge. Keep ahead a little downhill to cross a stile in the dip. Walk up the side of the next field with a hedge on your left and cross the stile at the top. The path descends once more, still with a hedge on the left. Directly ahead you will see Colmer's Hill crowned by a handful of pines. Continue up a slight rise to rejoin our outward bound route at point 2. Turn left to retrace your steps to the Ilchester Arms past the church which has a beautiful 'waggon head' barrel roof built by the shipwrights of West Bay. The school opposite the church, dated 1868, was given to the village by Gregory Raymond, rector of Symondsbury for 57 years.

PLACES OF INTEREST NEARBY

Bridport is an interesting market town with many picturesque side streets and alleyways. The **Museum** is housed in a 16th century building. Open daily between April and October 10 am to 5 pm, Sundays 2 pm to 5 pm; winter Wednesdays and Saturdays 10 am to 5 pm, Sundays 2 pm to 5 pm. Telephone: 01308 422116.

Melplash

THE VALE OF THE RIVER BRIT

The Half Moon Inn

MAP: OS EXPLORER 117 (GR 484976) — **WALK 2** — **DISTANCE:** 3 MILES

DIRECTIONS TO START: MELPLASH IS ABOUT 4 MILES NORTH OF BRIDPORT BESIDE THE A3066. APPROACHING FROM BRIDPORT, THE HALF MOON INN IS ON THE LEFT IMMEDIATELY AFTER YOU PASS THE CHURCH. **PARKING:** IN FRONT OF THE PUB OR IN THE CAR PARK AT THE SIDE NEAR THE CRICKET GROUND.

Although Melplash lies beside a busy road it is beautifully sited in one of West Dorset's loveliest places, the vale of the river Brit. This little river rises near Beaminster and flows south through Bridport to the sea, carving a valley where time seems to have stood still. Meadows are rich in wild flowers and wildlife finds shelter in the beech woods. Traffic noises are left behind as we take field and woodland paths to the open downland forming the valley's eastern slopes. We follow a raised path along the side of the downs with wide views over the valley before returning to the pub past the grounds of Melplash Court.

The Half Moon Inn

The Half Moon is a grey stone, thatched, old world pub. It has welcomed travellers for over 300 years. Hitching rings for your horse hang either side of the porch and you enter through a stable door. Inside the low-beamed bar and cosy restaurant you will find a warm family atmosphere, excellent ales and delicious home-cooked food. For a snack you might choose a sandwich, sausages with egg or fried onions, shell-on prawns or soup with crusty bread. Main meals might include 10oz steaks and salmon and broccoli pasta. Real ales are Palmers Bridport Bitter, IPA and 200 and Dorset Gold.

Perhaps it was over a mug of one of these ales that in the middle of the 19th century two farmers made a wager in the pub to compete in a ploughing match. This was the beginning of the Melplash Agricultural Society, formed in 1847 and one of the oldest in the country. Each year the Society holds a one-day agricultural show and a ploughing match. These days the show is held at Bridport on the last Thursday in August but all entrants for the various classes must live within 12 miles of Melplash church. A plaque on the wall of the pub garage commemorates the 150th anniversary of the founding of the Society.

Opening times at the Half Moon are from 12 noon to 3 pm and 6.30 to 11 pm (10.30 pm on Sundays). Food is served from 12 noon to 2 pm and 6.30 to 9 pm. There is a secluded garden. Telephone: 01308 488321.

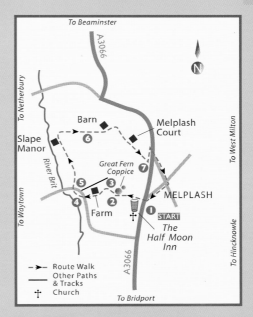

The Walk

① Leave the front porch of the pub and turn left, then almost immediately turn left again down a narrow lane running between the pub garden on the left and the cricket ground on the right. When the tarmac finishes keep straight on along a grassy path. Go through a gate and bearing very slightly left cross the field ahead to a stile.

② Cross the stile and follow a narrow path leading through the trees of Great Fern Coppice. The path bears gradually right to leave the woods over a stile. Now a splendid view of the valley of the river Brit opens before you.

③ Walk down the field keeping the hedge on your right and cross the next stile in front of some farm buildings. Turn immediately left for a few yards to a fence, then turn right past a wooden barrier down a narrow path with trees on your right. Lift

View of Melplash across the fields

the top bar to cross another barrier and keep ahead over the grass leaving all farm buildings on your right. Go through a gate, continue over a stile, then follow a path leading down over another stile to a lane.

④ Turn right and follow the lane past a footpath sign on the right, to a finger post on the right signed for Netherbury.

⑤ Turn right up a concrete track past some houses. The concrete gives way to a grassy track which leads through a gate to open downland. Follow the delightful path and after going through a gate look left for a glimpse of Georgian Slape Manor. The path descends and curves right. A hedge is down the slope on your left. After going through a gate the path becomes a wide sandy track which climbs a little then runs beside a hedge on the left.

⑥ Go through a gate and keep ahead beside a field. Pass a barn on the left and keep to the track as it hairpins left then right, still with a hedge on the left, round the edge of a field. Soon the hedge gives way to views of the grounds of Melplash Court and a glimpse of this Tudor manor. The track passes some thatched outbuildings and bring you to the main road, the A3066.

⑦ Turn left for about 60 yards then turn right to follow a quiet lane to a crossroads. Turn right again towards the tower of Melplash church directly ahead. As you near the end of the lane you will see the Half Moon Inn sign and you have completed your walk.

PLACES OF INTEREST NEARBY
Parnham House, the Tudor home of the John Makepeace Furniture Workshops, up the A3066 towards Beaminster. Café. Open from April to October. For details telephone: 01308 862204.

Nettlecombe

AN OLD WORLD VILLAGE HIDDEN IN THE HILLS

The Marquis of Lorne

MAP: OS EXPLORER 117 (GR 517957) | **WALK 3** | **DISTANCE:** 1½ OR 2½ MILES

DIRECTIONS TO START: NETTLECOMBE HAMLET IS ABOUT 4½ MILES NORTH-EAST OF BRIDPORT. TURN OFF THE A3066 BRIDPORT-BEAMINSTER ROAD ABOUT 1½ MILES NORTH OF BRIDPORT, FOLLOWING THE SIGN FOR LODERS. AT THE JUNCTION BEAR LEFT PAST MANGERTON MILL, DRIVE THROUGH WEST MILTON AND CONTINUE FOR A FURTHER MILE AND DRIVE STRAIGHT ACROSS A JUNCTION. THE MARQUIS OF LORNE IS ABOUT 300 YARDS FURTHER ON YOUR LEFT. **PARKING:** IN THE INN CAR PARK.

Nettlecombe is enchanting. This picturesque cluster of golden stone houses lies among the narrow sunken lanes of West Dorset at the foot of Eggardon, one of the area's highest hills, its summit encircled by the ramparts of an Iron Age fort. Apart from leading through glorious scenery both walks afford a fine view of Mappercombe Manor, a historic Tudor house with beautiful formal gardens. The longer walk visits Powerstock, another delightful old world village. The church has a richly carved 15th century south doorway and a fine Norman chancel arch.

The Marquis of Lorne

Once you have discovered this splendid inn you will definitely want to return. Originally a farmhouse, dating back to the 16th century, it offers a warm welcome to everyone, locals and visitors alike. The main bar, named after Eggardon, has blazing log fires in winter, mahogany panelling and walls decorated with a fascinating collection of old prints and photographs. There are two separate dining areas and a cosy snug also named after local hills. Among the many colourful characters who have loved this old inn was 'Big Bill'. He worked on the Bridport to Maiden Newton rail link and had hands as big as shovels, took size sixteen in boots and carried railway sleepers on his back. He liked to stand in the main bar and put one hand against the ceiling while the other was still resting on the floor!

Real ales are Palmers Bridport Bitter, IPA and 200. Dishes from the extensive menus could include 'Avocado Seafood', coq-au-vin, lamb chops marinated with apricots and rosemary and fresh crab. The inn opens 11.30 am to 2.30 pm and 6 pm to 11 pm. Food is served 11.30 am to 2 pm and 6.30 pm to 9 pm. On Sundays opening times are 12 noon to 3 pm and 7 pm to 10.30 pm with meals 12 noon to 2 pm and 7 pm to 9 pm.

Well-appointed accommodation is available and there is a self-catering cottage. The garden is beautiful with splendid views. Telephone: 01308 485236.

The Walk

① Leave the front door of the inn and turn left immediately down the lane to the village.

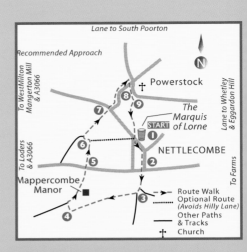

Pass a lane on the left, and the lane through the village signed as a no-through-road, and bear right uphill between high hedges.

② Walk straight over a crossing road and follow the track ahead. When the track curves left continue ahead for about 50 yards.

③ Leave the track here and turn right along a wide grassy path which runs at first between low hedges. The path continues along the foot of meadows which slope up to woods on your right. Go through a gate to walk along the top of a meadow with a hedge now on your right. Through the next gate the path crosses another meadow and leads through another gate. You have a glimpse of the gardens of Mappercombe Manor on your right followed by a thick beech hedge. When the beech hedge finishes keep ahead over the rough grass to the hedge on the opposite side of the meadow. (Ignore the footpath sign down the hill on your left.)

④ Go through a small gate and turn immediately right up the field with the hedge on your right, to meet a wide

The path to Powerstock village

for about 30 yards then turn right to follow a grassy path which tunnels steeply downhill, its high hedges framing Powerstock village on the hillside ahead. In the valley you meet a road.

⑦ Cross the road and follow the lane which climbs through Powerstock village to the Square. The church tower is on your right. Visit this wonderful church if you can and don't miss the 13th century dole table in the churchyard. Loaves were once placed here for distribution to the poor.

⑧ Turn sharp right in the Square, signed for Whetley and Eggardon Hill, with the church wall on your left. After about 60 yards the lane curves left.

⑨ Turn right at the finger post, signed for Nettlecombe, downhill to cross a footbridge and go through a gate. Bear slightly left over the meadow ahead to cross another footbridge and stile. A narrow path winds uphill through a gate to open downs. Walk uphill towards a fence on the corner of a wood. Continue with the fence on your left to cross a stile and go through a gate to the lane beside the Marquis of Lorne.

crossing track. Turn right and follow the track as it curves left past Mappercombe Manor. There is a lovely view of the house before the track runs through farm buildings to a lane.

⑤ Cross the lane, go through a gate and keep ahead beside fields with a hedge on your left to a crossing track.

For the shorter walk – which avoids the hilly lane into Powerstock – turn right here to follow the track to the lane directly opposite The Marquis of Lorne.

⑥ To continue the longer walk turn left

PLACES OF INTEREST NEARBY
Mangerton Mill, 17th century working water mill. Café. Opening times vary. For details telephone: 01308 485224.

Corscombe

A RIDGE WALK ON THE DOWNS

The Fox Inn

MAP: OS EXPLORER 117 (GR 526054)	WALK 4	DISTANCE: 3 MILES

DIRECTIONS TO START: CORSCOMBE IS A SMALL VILLAGE IN NORTH-WEST DORSET ABOUT 4 MILES NORTH-EAST OF BEAMINSTER. APPROACH VIA THE A356 CREWKERNE-DORCHESTER ROAD. IF APPROACHING FROM THE SOUTH TURN OFF THE A356 ALONG THE FIRST LANE ON THE RIGHT SIGNED FOR THE VILLAGE. COMING FROM THE NORTH PASS THE FIRST LANE ON THE LEFT SIGNED FOR CORSCOMBE AND TURN LEFT DOWN THE SECOND LANE SIGNED FOR THE VILLAGE. CONTINUE DOWNHILL FOR ABOUT A MILE KEEPING STRAIGHT AHEAD AT THE JUNCTION, FOLLOWING THE SIGN FOR THE FOX INN, WHICH APPEARS SHORTLY AFTER ON YOUR RIGHT.
PARKING: IN THE FOX INN'S NEW CAR PARK.

The West Dorset downs have been designated an area of outstanding natural beauty and after you have enjoyed this downland walk with its glorious views over rolling hills and thickly wooded valleys I am sure you will agree the area richly deserves that title. Corscombe is folded in a deep cleft in the hills and we take field and woodland paths to West Chelborough, surely one of the county's most secret and remote villages, lying in the shadow of a hill crowned with the earthworks of a medieval castle. A ridge path with panoramic views leads us back to Corscombe and the Fox Inn.

The Fox Inn

The Fox is a real country inn, its stone walls colour-washed a deep cream beneath a darkly thatched roof. Roses ramble round the porch in summer and blue and white checked curtains flutter from small casement windows. The building is at least 300 years old and inside it is just as you would expect with low ceilings, flagged floors and huge fireplaces crossed by massive blackened beams. There is a separate dining area as well as two cosy bars and a delightful conservatory. Real ales are Exmoor Ale, Summers Fox and London Pride. For a change you might try the Herefordshire cider or home-made elderflower cordial, damson vodka or sloe gin. The wine list is extensive and well chosen.

Interesting fish meals are a feature of the menu. These include herb-coated fillet of cod with red pesto and whole roast bream with tomato, olive and leek dressing. Other popular dishes are roast rack of Dorset lamb with rosemary gravy and venison with a damson and red wine sauce. Baguettes with ham or cheese and ploughman's lunches are served at the bar.

Opening times are 12 noon to 3 pm and 7 pm to 11 pm. Meals are served from 12 noon to 2 pm and 7 pm to 9 pm (9.30 pm on Fridays and Saturdays). Bed and breakfast accommodation is available. Telephone: 01935 891330.

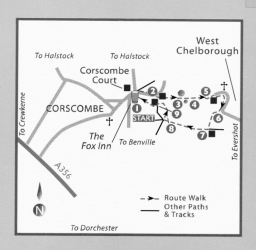

The Walk

① Turn right from the front of the inn down the lane and after about 100 yards turn right along a narrow lane signed as a no-through-road.

② When the lane curves left in front of Norwood Cottage keep ahead along a footpath to the right of the cottage and go through a gate into a wood. Follow the woodland path through a gate to an open area. The path is faint but keep straight ahead to go through a gate into another wood. The path ahead dips over a stream to lead through a gate to another open area.

③ The path is not clear but keep straight ahead across the field to go through a gate into a third wood. A narrow path directly under a line of power cables leads through a gate to open fields.

④ Keep ahead to walk up to the next gate. Go through the gate and bearing very slightly right cross the grass to go through a gate in the opposite hedge leading into the yard of Dairy House Farm.

⑤ Keep ahead for a few yards then bear left, leaving the farm buildings and a row of cottages on your right, to a tarmac lane in West Chelborough. Visit the charming little church – which you come to on your left – if you have time. Among its treasures

17

East Chelborough hill

⑦ Turn right before the gate to follow a grassy ridge track along the top of fields and through gates for about ½ mile to a junction of five ways. (NB one of the footpaths is blocked and not visible.)

⑧ Turn right down a stony hedged track. Go through the gate and walk down the field ahead, hedge on the right, to go through a small gate into a wood. Take the woodland path which leads through a gate to a meadow. Keep straight on, hedge on the left, to a gate with a house a few yards ahead.

⑨ Go through the gate then turn immediately left over a stile. Cross a small plank bridge and turn right to pass the house and grounds on your right and cross another stile. A tree-shaded path then leads to meadows. Follow the narrow path over the grass towards the thatched roof of the Fox Inn. A final gate brings you to the track to the right of the inn.

is a richly carved 12th century font. Continue along the lane which curves right and climbs for about ¼ mile.

⑥ When the lane swings sharply left, turn right along a concrete track over a cattle grid and through a gate. Follow the track as it rises to give glorious views. The track slopes downhill to a gate before a yard with a barn on the left.

PLACES OF INTEREST NEARBY

Beaminster, to the south-west, is a picturesque market town. South of the town Tudor **Parnham House**, the home of the John Makepeace Furniture Workshops, is open from April to October. Café. For more details telephone: 01308 862204.

Evershot

HARDY'S WORLD AND MELBURY PARK

The Acorn Inn

MAP: OS EXPLORER 117 (GR 574045)　　**WALK 5**　　**DISTANCE:** 4 MILES

DIRECTIONS TO START: EVERSHOT IS A SMALL VILLAGE MIDWAY BETWEEN YEOVIL AND DORCHESTER. APPROACH VIA THE A37, TAKE THE TURNING FOR EVERSHOT AND CONTINUE FOR ABOUT 1½ MILES TO THE ACORN INN WHICH IS ON YOUR RIGHT. **PARKING:** IN THE ACORN CAR PARK.

The route of this walk runs almost entirely through the parkland surrounding Melbury House. It is an open landscape of green hills and valleys set with magnificent plantations of trees. The park and the fine house it surrounds were acquired in 1500 by Henry Strangways. His son, Sir Giles, rebuilt and extended the property and in the 18th century part of the building was remodelled in the classical style. Today the Strangways family still own Melbury House. In August 2000 they celebrated five hundred years of residence with a huge party for the people in the neighbouring villages.

Our walk begins from Evershot, close to the southern gate of the park, and follows paths and lanes to give a fine view of Melbury House. We return through the Deer Park. Red deer predominate but you may also spot fallow, Sika and Père David deer, a rare Chinese species.

The Acorn Inn

Immortalised by Thomas Hardy as 'The Sow-and-Acorn' in his novel *Tess of the d'Urbervilles*, this mellow stone-built inn is one of Dorset's most delightful hostelries. Here you will receive a warm and friendly welcome and enjoy the peaceful atmosphere of a traditional country inn. Bar areas include the attractive 'Village Bar', a cosy room set with small tables painted by a local artist with a variety of games and walls hung with lively portraits. This favoured spot is the haunt of the inn's ghost, the mysterious 'Lady in Grey'. A safer resort might be the restaurant with its splendid Ham stone fireplaces.

Real ales are Butcombe Bitter, London Pride and Palmers Best Bitter and there is a choice of well-selected wines. Special delights on offer are home-made elderflower cordial, sloe gin and damson vodka. The usual bar meals are available and a variety of tempting dishes could include wild boar sausages, venison with red wine and juniper sauce and honey-roasted duck breast.

Opening hours are 11.30 am to 11 pm and meals are served 12 noon to 2 pm and 7 pm to 9.30 pm. Excellent accommodation is provided in rooms called after Thomas Hardy's names for Dorset villages. Telephone: 01935 83228.

The Walk

① Turn left from the entrance to the inn to walk through the village. No two houses are alike in Evershot. Some reflect the 17th century with their mullioned windows and arched doorways, others are small and thatched.

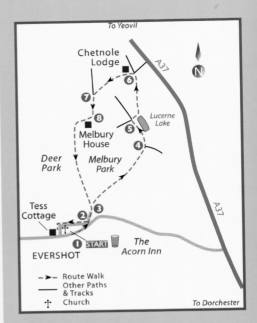

② When the main road curves right keep straight on, leaving a stone seat beneath a large tree on your right, and follow the lane up the private drive – footpath only – into Melbury Park.

③ After about 150 yards take the joining lane on the right leading uphill. The lane becomes a gravel track and emerges from the trees at the top of the hill to reveal a fine view over the valley to the wooded slopes of Bubb Down. Follow the track downhill over all crosstracks to a crossing track at the foot of the hillside.

④ Turn left following the sign 'Mel. Osm.' (Melbury Osmond). On your right you will catch glimpses of Lucerne Lake and as you near the northern end of the lake you have a better view of the water with a thatched boathouse beside it. The track begins to curve right.

The thatched boathouse beside Lucerne Lake in Melbury Park

⑤ Leave the main track here which continues uphill and turn sharp right round the head of the lake. (Look for a bridleway sign just round the corner.) Continue over a bridge and keep ahead beside a field with a fence on your right to go through a small gate in the far corner. Bear left beneath the trees to meet a tarmac lane.

⑥ Turn left, leaving Chetnole Lodge on your right, to walk through the park. Continue past a cottage on your left to follow the lane to a T-junction.

⑦ Turn left towards the impressive north front of Melbury House. Thomas Hardy set many of the scenes in the first edition of his novel *The Woodlanders* in this area. He called the great house 'King's Hintock Court'. Giles Winterborne, an evicted villager, is forced to make his home in 'One-Chimney Hut' in the woods nearby.

⑧ The lane swings right through gates to cross the Deer Park. Continue along the lane to leave Melbury Park and rejoin our outward-bound route at point 3. Retrace your steps past the seat and tree and after a few yards turn right to follow Back Lane which finally curves left. The lane meets the main road between the church on your left and the cottage where Hardy's Tess stopped for breakfast on your right. Turn left to return to the Acorn.

PLACES OF INTEREST NEARBY

Although Melbury House is not open there is a programme of **guided walks** which provide more extensive access to the park, much of which is a site of Special Scientific Interest. For information send a s.a.e. marked 'Guided Walks' to: Ilchester Estates, The Estate Office, Evershot, Dorchester, Dorset DT2 OJY.

Thornford

A RAMBLE THROUGH THE VALE OF BLACKMOOR
The King's Arms Inn

MAP: OS EXPLORER 129 (GR 604131)	**WALK 6**	DISTANCE: 3 MILES

DIRECTIONS TO START: THORNFORD IS A SMALL VILLAGE ABOUT 4 MILES SOUTH-WEST OF SHERBORNE. THE BEST APPROACH IS VIA THE A352 SHERBORNE-DORCHESTER ROAD. TURN FOR THE VILLAGE OFF THE A352 AND CONTINUE FOR ABOUT 3 MILES TO THE KING'S ARMS WHICH IS ON YOUR RIGHT. **PARKING:** IN THE KING'S ARMS CAR PARK OR IN THE VILLAGE.

Thornford is a village with a secret! You will find it tucked away among the winding lanes and low wooded hills in the north of the Blackmoor Vale and, like so many Dorset villages, it is a charming mix of stone-built houses and cottages. But leave your car and walk up the lane by the church and you will discover what makes Thornford so special. The village is built along the crest of a hill and a glorious view stretches before you far over the valley of the river Yeo to the Somerset hills. This is the highlight of this gentle stroll but there is much more to enjoy. We cross the river and head west to visit Bradford Abbas, a beautiful village with a magnificent 15th century church. Pleasant field paths lead back to Thornford.

The King's Arms Inn

Superbly situated at the top of the village street beside Thornford's well-known Jubilee clock tower, the King's Arms is a friendly village pub offering a typical warm Dorset welcome to all. The inn dates from 1905, built, according to the lease, on 'the site of a carpenter's yard and shop and the garden and premises thereunto adjoining'. So there is plenty of room outside for a delightful garden with a raised patio and a safe play area for children. Inside there is a cosy bar and a separate lounge and comfortable dining area. Old prints of the village decorate the walls and don't miss the talented landlady's fine pencil sketch of a farm which stands in one of the fireplaces.

Real ales include Badger Best and IPA and wines are available by the glass. The menu offers an extensive range of home-cooked meals, bar snacks and a specials board – examples are home-cooked ham served with onion rings, mushrooms and fried egg, steak, kidney and mushroom pie and sweet and sour chicken cooked in butter with a hint of garlic. For a sweet you might be tempted by a banana split or hot chocolate fudge cake.

Opening times are 12 noon to 2.30 pm and 7 pm to 11 pm (10.30 pm on Sundays). Meals are served 12 noon to 2 pm and 7 pm to 9 pm. There are no evening meals on Sunday and Monday and the inn is closed Tuesday lunchtimes. The King's Arms is a small family-run inn so if you plan a group visit it is a good idea to order your meal before your walk. Telephone: 01935 872294.

The Walk

① Turn right from the front of the King's Arms along Church Road past the clock tower built to commemorate the 60th year of the reign of Queen Victoria. Pass the Old School House on your left and continue to a T-junction. Bear left for about 150 yards.

② Turn left down Bembury Lane. This pleasant little lane curves right past Bembury Farm and becomes a grassy track leading ahead through trees to a wooden footbridge over the Yeo. Cross the bridge and two smaller bridges and go through a small iron gate to a field.

③ Keep ahead along the grassy path beside the field, hedge on the right. The path bears right through a gate. Bear left to cross the next field with a hedge about 40 yards away on your left. Go over a stile and walk towards the railway crossing gate, passing the thatched barn of medieval Wyke Farm on your right.

④ Just before the crossing gate turn left to

The path past Wyke Farm

walk along the edge of fields through gates with the railway on your right to meet a road.

⑤ Turn left down the road then turn right following the sign for Bradford Abbas to explore this lovely village.

To continue the walk turn left (right if you are coming from the village) over an iron stile along the narrow path running between stone walls opposite the post office. A gate opens to meadows bordering the Yeo. Bear left with a stone wall at first on your left and go through a gate to rejoin the road.

⑥ Cross straight over and follow the track ahead. Continue along the right-hand track at the division. Turn right in front of the former Mill House through a gate into a meadow. Bear left along the raised path beside a stream – fence on the left – and cross a wooden footbridge over the Yeo. Follow the path straight ahead over a field and go through a gate. The path now bears half-right across the next field to go through a gate with the corner of a hedge a few yards away on the left. Cross the field ahead aiming for Thornford church tower on the hill.

⑦ After the next gate climb the hill to the tower on your left. Look back for the splendid view! A narrow path leads to the approach to the church, well worth a visit. Among some fragments of 15th century glass in the south-east window in the chancel you will see 'a sparrow with a harrow' commemorating a certain Dr Sparrow, vicar of Sherborne about 1419. Walk down to the road and turn right to return to the King's Arms.

PLACES OF INTEREST NEARBY

Sherborne with its magnificent abbey and two castles is only a short drive away.

Puncknowle

IN THE VALLEY OF THE RIVER BRIDE

The Crown Inn

MAP: OS OUTDOOR LEISURE 15 (GR 535887) **WALK 7** **DISTANCE:** 1¾ MILES

DIRECTIONS TO START: THE BEST APPROACH TO PUNCKNOWLE IS VIA THE B3157, THE COAST ROAD BETWEEN BRIDPORT AND ABBOTSBURY. TURN OFF THE B3157 FOR PUNCKNOWLE IN SWYRE AND IN ABOUT ½ MILE TURN RIGHT FOR PUNCKNOWLE VILLAGE. THE CROWN INN IS ON THE LEFT. **PARKING:** THE CROWN INN CAR PARK (WITH PERMISSION) OR ROADSIDE PARKING OPPOSITE.

Although this walk is short I think you will find it very rewarding. You will discover a village straight from a Thomas Hardy novel with church and manor overlooking a street of thatched cottages built of cream coloured local stone and enjoy magnificent sea views. Puncknowle lies in the valley of the river Bride sheltered from the sea by a downland ridge. From Puncknowle we climb the downs to the foot of The Knoll, an isolated hill which has lent its name to the village. A short climb brings you to the coastguards' former look-out to share their view far over Chesil Bank and Lyme Bay to the great line of cliffs rolling westward into Devon. An attractive path past the manor and church leads back to the village.

The Crown Inn

The 16th century Crown Inn is a traditional Dorset pub with beamed ceilings, comfortable wooden settles and huge fireplaces. A friendly resident ghost occasionally makes an appearance in the oldest part of the building. Evidently she is a former landlady still keeping a watchful eye on what goes on! We can well understand her reluctance to leave. Most of the food is home-cooked with generous additions of alcohol – for example, steak and kidney pie cooked in Guinness, beef and parsnip casserole cooked in Palmers beer and chicken and cranberry casserole in red wine. Then there are lighter meals such as prawns in filo pastry served with black bean dip. A full range of bar snacks is available too.

Real ales are Palmers Bridport Bitter, IPA, Tally Ho! and 200. Cider is Taunton Traditional and wines include a French house wine and a special for each month.

Meals are served 12 noon to 2 pm (2.30 pm on Sunday) and 7 pm to 9.30 pm in the evening. Drinking hours are until 11 pm. Families are welcome and have a special room and dogs are welcome in the bar areas. There is a delightful garden with views over the valley. The inn also offers accommodation. Telephone: 01308 897711.

The Walk

① Turn left from the entrance to the Crown to walk along the village street past the gates to the manor gardens on your right. Shortly you come to the junction of Looke Lane on your left and Clay Lane on your right. Do not take either lane but look for an arrow on a post indicating a footpath

through a farm entrance on the right opposite the Looke Lane turning.

② Turn right following this sign to walk past some farm buildings. You pass two further barns on your left. The track climbs gently to meet Clay Lane.

③ Bear right up Clay Lane. As you gain height you enjoy wide views over the Bride valley and the picturesque village of Litton Cheney on the opposite hillside, almost enclosed within one of the rounded bowl-shaped coombes typical of West Dorset. Pass a footpath sign on the right – this is our return route – and continue to a gate and stile on the right with a marker stone 'Footpath to Knoll'.

④ Turn right to follow the white track uphill. The track curves right to the coastguards' former look-out crowning the top of the hill. The small stone-built hut has recently been restored as part of a Millennium project. From the windswept grasses and cornfields surrounding the hut the view is really breathtaking.

The old preaching cross in the churchyard opposite the inn

return route is delightful! Continue down the field with a hedge on your right to cross a stile. Keep ahead down the next field and step over a stone stile to walk down a narrow field between hedges and cross a final stile. The path drops more steeply now beside trees on the right then over the grass to tunnel beneath trees to a small wooden gate. Go through the gate past a magnificent chestnut tree on the left to a crossing track. Turn right to walk down to the road leading into Puncknowle and turn right again to return to the Crown Inn and your car.

The church of St Mary opposite the inn is well worth a visit. Most of the building dates from the 12th century including the simple chancel arch surmounted by the remains of medieval wall paintings. The massive entrance door in the north wall bears nail studs forming the initials 'RN' for Robert Napier (his family owned the manor until 1710) and a gilded 17th century helmet which formerly carried the Napier crest hangs on the wall of the nave. Over the church wall you can catch a glimpse of the manor described by Frederick Treves in *Highways and Byways in Dorset* as 'a marvel of ancient dignity and peace'.

⑤ Retrace your steps down The Knoll to Clay Lane and turn left to walk down to the footpath sign on the left signed for Puncknowle.

⑥ Leave your outward-bound route here and turn left along the wide track which brings you to a gate. Through the gate turn right, signed 'Knackers Hole' – a most misleading name in our opinion as this

PLACES OF INTEREST NEARBY

The Chesil Bank and **Abbotsbury village, Swannery and Gardens** – see Walks 4 and 11.

Abbotsbury

A COASTAL WALK IN THE STEPS OF THE MONKS

The Ilchester Arms

MAP: OS OUTDOOR LEISURE 15 (GR 575854)   **WALK 8**   **DISTANCE:** 2 MILES

DIRECTIONS TO START: ABBOTSBURY LIES BESIDE THE B3157 ABOUT 8 MILES WEST OF WEYMOUTH. APPROACHING FROM THE EAST DRIVE INTO THE VILLAGE AND FOLLOW THE B3157 AS IT TURNS RIGHT FOR BRIDPORT. AFTER ONLY A FEW YARDS TURN SHARP LEFT UNDER THE ARCHED ENTRANCE TO THE ILCHESTER ARMS' CAR PARK. **PARKING:** THE ILCHESTER ARMS' CAR PARK. HAVE A WORD WITH ONE OF THE STAFF BEFORE LEAVING YOUR CAR WHILE YOU WALK.

The mellow stone and thatch village of Abbotsbury, set comfortably in a sheltered hollow of the coastal downs at the western end of the Fleet, is one of Dorset's gems. But in spite of its many visitors this beautiful and historic village has remained remarkably unspoilt. A Benedictine abbey was founded here in the 11th century and although little can be seen of the ruins today the magnificent thatched tithe barn, the hilltop chapel of St Catherine and the Swannery, originally established by the monks, have survived. They are now cared for by the Strangways family who took over the estate at the Dissolution. All these can be enjoyed on this walk which also includes part of the Dorset Coast Path.

The Ilchester Arms

This historic former coaching inn stands on the site of an ancient hostelry established by the monks of the nearby abbey. The present building dates back 300 years and behind the Georgian façade you will find the beamed ceilings, wood panelling and huge inglenook fireplaces of an earlier age. The atmosphere is particularly restful and you will receive the same warm welcome that I am sure greeted Queen Victoria when she spent a night here.

But this is an inn that has kept up with the times and a delightful modern feature is the large sunny conservatory. Here and in the bar and restaurant you can enjoy country cooking at its best. Apart from bar snacks which might include marinated steak baguettes with mushrooms and cheese and smoked bacon salad with tomato salsa, examples of the wide range of dishes on the menu are smooth Dorset pâté, Scottish salmon fillet with watercress sauce, and home-made steak, kidney and mushroom pie. Among the specials when we called were deep fried whitebait with paprika and the splendid 'Ilchester mixed grill'. Real ales are Bass, 6X and Flowers.

Opening times in summer are 11 am to 11 pm; the rest of the year 11 am to 3 pm (11.30 am on Mondays) and 6 pm to 11 pm. Food is served 12 noon to 2.30 pm and 6.30 pm to 9 pm. Excellent accommodation is available. Telephone: 01305 871243.

The Walk

① Leave the front porch of the Ilchester Arms and turn left up the village street.

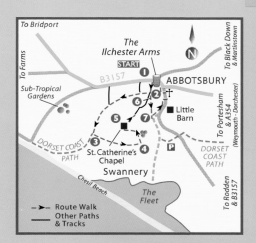

After about 60 yards turn left again, signed for Chapel Hill, the Swannery and Chesil Beach. The way becomes a pleasant track with beautiful views over Abbotsbury with St Catherine's Chapel crowning the hill ahead.

② The track runs to a gate. Turn right before the gate, signed 'Chesil Beach', round the foot of the hill which is on your left. At the next signpost ignore a track on the right and keep ahead, still following the sign for Chesil Beach. The sandy track winds gently downhill between high hedges and leads through a gate. Continue following the Chesil Beach sign past another track on the right. Below the woods on your right the downland is terraced into strip lynchets which date from medieval times. The track curves south and you will see the ridge of Chesil Beach ahead. Continue to a signpost and stile on the left.

③ Turn left over the stile, signed for the coast path and Swannery, and climb the terraced hillside to meet a fence on the right. Now follow the coast path for about ¾ mile with splendid views of the Fleet and later the trees surrounding the Swannery on your right.

Abbotsbury

④ As the path begins to dip look for a marker stone on the left indicating a path uphill to St Catherine's Chapel. Turn left and climb up to a small wood on your right. Now bear half-left to climb to the highest point and cross the grass to the chapel. Built in the 15th century by the monks as a seamark and chantry for sailors the chapel is built entirely of stone.

⑤ Leave by the north entrance, go through a swing gate and follow the path downhill. The path bears right with a stone wall on the left then continues downhill to the gate at point 2.

⑥ Before the gate turn sharp right, signed for the Swannery. Follow the path over a stream and cross a stone stile over a wall to a lane.

⑦ If you wish you could turn right here to visit the Swannery then retrace your steps up the lane. If not, turn left and follow the lane to a road. Bear left to the tithe barn then continue up the lane for just a few yards. Turn right to climb the path past the abbey ruins to the church which is full of interest. Leave by the north porch and turn right to the main street of the village. Turn left to the Ilchester Arms.

PLACES OF INTEREST NEARBY

Tithe Barn Museum. Open all week from 10 am to 6 pm between Easter and October. For details of other times telephone: 01305 871817.

The Swannery is open from early March to the end of October, every day between 10 am and 6 pm. Telephone: 01305 871684.

Sub-Tropical Gardens – open every day, 10 am to 6 pm between March and October, rest of year 4 pm. Telephone: 01305 871387.

Langton Herring

THE FLEET – A WILDLIFE HAVEN

The Elm Tree Inn

MAP: OS OUTDOOR LEISURE 15 (GR 614825) **WALK 9** **DISTANCE:** 2½ MILES

DIRECTIONS TO START: LANGTON HERRING IS A SMALL VILLAGE A MILE WEST OF THE B3157. LEAVE THE B3157 FOLLOWING THE SIGN FOR THE VILLAGE, THEN TURN LEFT FOLLOWING THE SIGN FOR THE ELM TREE INN WHICH IS ON YOUR RIGHT. **PARKING:** THE ELM TREE INN HAS SET ASIDE A LARGE PARKING AREA – THE PADDOCK – FOR PATRONS WHO WISH TO WALK. TURN RIGHT TOWARDS THE INN THEN IMMEDIATELY RIGHT AGAIN INTO THE PADDOCK.

The Dorset coastline is famous for its towering pinnacles of chalk, the bays and inlets of its clay cliffs and the great limestone rampart of the Purbeck peninsula but this remarkable coast has another claim to fame, a feature unique in Europe. This is the Chesil Bank, an immense beach of shingle smoothed and shaped by the sea running east for 19 miles from West Bay to Portland. Trapped behind it lie the sheltered waters of the Fleet, 8 miles in length and the largest lagoon in Britain. Most is now a nature reserve and a marvellous place to observe wildlife, especially in winter when it becomes a haven for migratory birds. To appreciate the remoteness and mystery of this very special part of Dorset follow the route of this walk from a quiet village tucked behind a ridge in the downs to the shores of the Fleet. Remember your binoculars!

The Elm Tree Inn

This bright, attractive inn is beautifully situated beside a very pretty garden surrounded by trees. From the outside the building appears quite recent but part of the inn dates from the 16th century and has many tales to tell of smuggling days. As in most villages close to the Dorset coast, the inhabitants of Langton Herring took an active part in the lucrative trade in smuggled goods from France during the 18th and early 19th centuries and a bricked-up hole in the Elm Tree Inn cellar is possibly an escape tunnel or a hiding place for their illicit brandy and tea, tobacco, laces and silks. Low beamed ceilings, a huge inglenook fireplace and walls decorated with shining brass and copper contribute to the pleasant, relaxed atmosphere of this delightful inn.

Real ales are 6X, Bass and Flowers and the cider is Blackthorn. The menu is so extensive that everyone must surely find a dish to suit. Specialities include Elm Tree Mustard Chicken, Langton Beefsteak and Ale Pie and Baked Cod Mornay and if you fancy something more exotic you could sample Cantonese Black Duck with black cherries and black bean sauce.

Opening times on Monday to Saturday are 11.30 am to 3 pm and 6.30 pm to 11.30 pm. Sunday hours are 12 noon to 3 pm and 7 pm to 10.30 pm. Food is served 12 noon to 2 pm and 7 pm to 9 pm. Telephone: 01305 871257.

The Walk

① Turn right from the entrance to the inn and almost immediately turn right again to

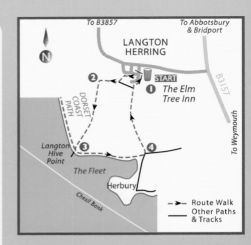

pass the little church of St Peter with its Saxon tower on your right. The lane curves right then left past a turning on the right to a T-junction. Turn left up the part-gravel, part-tarmac track and follow it as it bears right along a high ridge with wide views over a downland valley on your right and glimpses of the sea ahead.

② Keep to the lane as it curves left to give you your first view of the Fleet protected by the biscuit-coloured ridge of the Chesil Bank. More splendid views unfold to the east as the track descends past a small wood on the left then bears right past the garages of a line of coastguards' cottages to the footpath sign for the Dorset Coast Path. Continue past the sign down the slipway to the beach at Langton Hive Point. Now you look straight across the lagoon to the Chesil Bank, home for many rare birds including the little tern which nests among the pebbles. This small bird is a delight to watch as it hovers over the water, slender wings arched above its back, before diving to catch a tiny fish in its black-tipped beak.

Retrace your steps to the 'Coast Path' signpost.

Langton Hive Point beside the Fleet

③ Turn right following the sign for the Fleet and Weymouth. The path traces the foot of a field with the Fleet on your right, then tunnels through some bushes to bring you to open fields once more. Across the water we saw herons fishing below the low cliffs of Herbury peninsula. The path runs beside tall stands of rushes and spiky clumps of teasels and sea holly to lead over a stile and across a narrow footbridge to a signpost.

④ Turn left for Langton Herring and follow the track as it climbs the low hill head past an enormous yew tree on the left. The path levels as it approaches the rooftops of the village. Go through a metal gate and down the track to a lane. Turn right and follow the lane as it curves left to bring you back to the Elm Tree Inn on your left.

PLACES OF INTEREST NEARBY

Weymouth has many attractions to offer the visitor apart from its picturesque harbour and beach. On **Brewers' Quay** you can enjoy the fascinating 'Timewalk' experience through 600 years of history and visit **The Shopping Village**. Telephone: 01305 777622. The Victorian **Nothe Fort** has been restored and opened to the public and is surrounded by beautiful gardens. Telephone: 01305 787243.

Portland

A UNIQUE LANDSCAPE

The Pulpit Inn

MAP: OS OUTDOOR LEISURE 15 (GR 678688) **WALK 10** **DISTANCE:** 3 MILES

DIRECTIONS TO START: FOLLOW THE A354 SOUTH THROUGH WEYMOUTH, CROSS TO PORTLAND AND CONTINUE THROUGH FORTUNESWELL, KEEPING TO THE A354 AS FAR AS EASTON. NOW FOLLOW THE BROWN SIGNS FOR PORTLAND BILL. THE PULPIT INN IS ON YOUR RIGHT **PARKING:** IN THE PULPIT INN CAR PARK.

Portland is a world apart with its own distinctive landscape. Until the construction of a bridge in 1839 only a narrow bank of pebbles, the Chesil Bank, linked this 4½ mile long block of limestone with the mainland. Isolated, and surrounded by inaccessible sheer-sided cliffs which protected them like the walls of a medieval fortress, the Portlanders developed their own independent customs and lifestyle, changing only slowly with the centuries. In some areas large open fields and meadows are still divided into strips as they were in Saxon days. You will see some of these fields, called on Portland 'lawns', as you follow the route of this walk. And there is much more to enjoy as we take the coast path from the Pulpit Rock round Portland Bill. In addition to splendid sea views, you will discover a wealth of birdlife, butterflies and wild flowers.

The Pulpit Inn

This large inn, built in 1954 of the local white limestone, stands high with a fine view over Portland Bill lighthouse to the Channel. It is, I was informed, quite literally at the 'Top of the Bill'! Inside it is spacious and airy with separate bar areas and restaurant and plenty of room for families. Here you are assured of a friendly welcome in warm and comfortable surroundings.

If you like your fish really fresh then you have a treat in store! It is brought to the inn daily straight off the boats. There is a wide choice of 'Seafood Specials' including Portland crab salad, fresh plaice fillet and lemon sole. Among the meat and poultry dishes are a 'Sizzling Skillet Combination' – slices of fillet steak and chicken breast marinated with peppers and onions – and half a honey-roasted duck served with orange sauce. Bar snacks include home-made soup, a variety of ploughman's lunches and home-made steak and kidney pie. The Sunday carvery is deservedly popular and it is a good plan to book your table in advance. Real ales are Bass, Tetley Best Bitter and Morland Old Speckled Hen. Cider is Blackthorn and there is a well-chosen wine list.

Tables on the patio overlooking the coast are the perfect place to enjoy a drink on a warm summer's evening while the children enjoy themselves in the sanded play area nearby. The Pulpit Inn also offers accommodation. Telephone: 01305 821237.

The Walk

① Turn right from the inn entrance to

follow the road for just a few yards. When the road curves left keep straight on along the lane marked 'Private Road' to double footpath signs. Turn left, signed 'Coast Path', over the grass. The Lighthouse and Visitor Centre are beyond a large car park on your left. Bear right round the edge of an abandoned quarry then follow the track which descends to run west through the quarry to meet the coast path (an inconspicuous marker stone is on your right). Beyond the path the coast shelves to the Pulpit Rock, a forbidding mass of limestone defying the force of the waves. It has always been associated with the smuggling of luxury goods during the 18th and 19th centuries and marks the entrance to several caves.

② Turn left to follow the coast path past the white sea-marker inscribed 'T.H.' (Trinity House) on your right and the Lighthouse on your left. Not far off the coast the white crested waves of the infamous Portland Race tumble over the 2 mile long Shambles Sandbank which lies just beneath the surface. Continue along the eastern coast path past the beach huts and a track on the left for about a mile when you will see the

Pulpit Rock on a calm day

dark entrance of a large cave. In the bowl-shaped hollow over the grass on your left there is a metal grill revealing the interior of the cave. Continue along the path for about 100 yards to another abandoned quarry with a hoist on the cliff edge.

③ Bear left along a track, leaving the quarry on your right, to meet the road.

④ Turn left along the pavement for about ¼ mile passing a footpath sign on the right.

⑤ Turn right at the next footpath sign (no stile or gate) to follow a track a little uphill. On your left you have a splendid view over the Portland lawns. The track doglegs left then right beside open meadows to reach a stone wall. Here it curves left with the wall on the right and runs to meet the coast path on the western side of the island.

⑥ Bear left to follow the coast path past the former Upper Lighthouse on your left. Look back to enjoy the view of the Dorset coastline. The path curves a little left past the Coastguard Station to a tarmac lane. Cross straight over and walk down the grass ahead to the Pulpit Inn.

PLACES OF INTEREST NEARBY

Portland Bill Lighthouse, Visitor Centre and Exhibition are open from April to the end of September, 11 am to 5 pm; closed on Saturdays. Telephone: 01305 820495.

The Bird Observatory and Field Centre are housed in the former Lower Lighthouse. Visitors are welcome and there is hostel accommodation. Telephone: 01305 820553.

Portland Castle, dating from 1593, overlooking Portland Harbour. Open April to October, 10 am to 6 pm (or dusk if earlier). Telephone: 01305 820539.

Charminster

WHERE THE CERNE MEETS THE FROME

The Three Compasses

MAP: OS EXPLORER 117 (GR 678928) — **WALK 11** — **DISTANCE:** 2 MILES

DIRECTIONS TO START: CHARMINSTER IS ABOUT 2 MILES NORTH OF DORCHESTER. APPROACHING FROM THE EAST AND SOUTH TAKE THE A37 YEOVIL ROAD. TURN RIGHT ALONG THE A352, SIGNED 'CHARMINSTER', DRIVE INTO THE VILLAGE THEN TURN LEFT UP WEST HILL, SIGNED 'MAIDEN NEWTON' TO THE PUB WHICH IS ON YOUR LEFT. FROM THE WEST, LEAVE THE A37 SIGNED 'CHARMINSTER'. THE PUB IS ON YOUR RIGHT. **PARKING:** IN THE PUB CAR PARK.

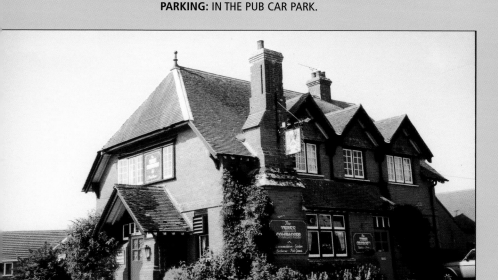

The little river Cerne carves one of the most beautiful of Dorset's downland valleys as it flows south to meet the Frome near Dorchester. Charminster is an enchanting village lying on each side of the Cerne close to the meeting place of the two rivers. We begin this walk with a stroll through the oldest part of the village past rows of thatched cottages and houses, some with cob walls and others banded with flint and stone. Beside the Cerne stands the church of St Mary the Virgin, famous for its magnificent tower built of warm red Ham Hill stone early in the 15th century. A path from the churchyard leads over the river to head north along the crest of the hill with splendid views over the valley. We descend to recross the river and take meadow paths back to the Three Compasses pub.

The Three Compasses

This village pub was built in 1915 on the site of a much older inn beside the steep descent of West Hill, once the main road between Yeovil and Dorchester. It stands in 'The Square' beside a row of attractive Georgian cottages. Inside, the atmosphere is friendly and welcoming with comfortable red plush window seats and bar stools. Separate from the main bar area you will find a pleasant 'snug' decorated with colourful china. Tetley's real ale is on tap and for a change you could sample one of the country wines. A wide range of bar meals is available ranging from ploughman's – try the tasty local ham! – and jacket potatoes with an interesting list of fillings, to a tempting moussaka. Cider is Blackthorn.

Opening times every day are 12 noon to 3 pm and 5 pm to 11 pm. It is a splendid pub for walkers as it doesn't matter what time you would like to eat. Food is served throughout opening hours so you can stop and enjoy the view on your walk without fear of missing your meal!

Drinks can be enjoyed outside in the garden and bed and breakfast accommodation is available. Telephone: 01305 263618.

The Walk

① Leave the front of the pub and turn right down West Hill. Cross the A352 and walk down the lane ahead which curves left then right to the church. Immediately after the last house on the left, turn left through a small wooden gate to walk over the churchyard to the south porch. There is a great deal to enjoy inside this historic

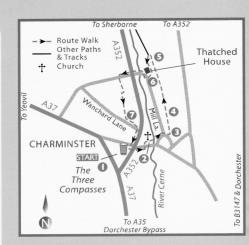

building. Arcades of sturdy 12th century columns either side of the nave support pointed arches with neat nail-head ornament, part of the stone stairway to a former roodloft has been preserved and there are many interesting monuments.

② With the south porch on your left continue over the churchyard to a signpost pointing left for Mill Lane. Turn left to leave the churchyard through a gate opening to the riverbank. Bear right over the wooden footbridge and keep ahead to pass a lane on the left. Continue uphill for about 100 yards.

③ Just before the road begins to curve right look for a very narrow path on the left running past some concrete garages. Turn left to follow this to a signpost and bear left following the sign for Herrison. A pleasant leafy path leads you along the hillside with glimpses of the rooftops of Charminster in the valley on your left.

④ The path divides in front of a small gate and a sign 'Princes Plot – Nature and Picnic area'. Take the right-hand path to

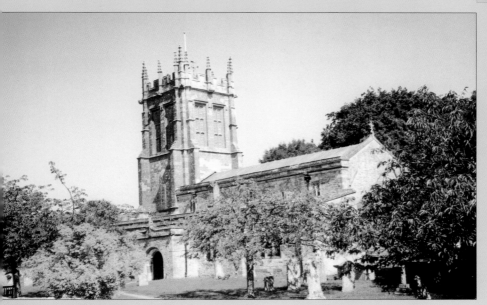

Charminster's lovely church

keep your height. Cross a stile to leave the trees and emerge on the open hillside. Keep ahead along the top of the meadow with a hedge on your right to go through an iron gate. Follow the narrow path ahead which traces the hillside to a signpost.

⑤ Our route is indicated by the sign for Mill Lane but no path is visible! However, bear half-left diagonally down the hillside towards a prominent thatched house at the foot. Pass the house on your right and immediately turn right through a gate to Mill Lane.

⑥ Bear right and follow the track round to the left to cross a footbridge over the Cerne. Continue to cross the A352 and walk up the lane ahead past Highfield Close. Turn left following the sign for Wanchard Lane. Cross the stile and walk beside a field, hedge on the left. After crossing double stiles the path turns right over another set of double stiles and then bears left to resume its original heading. Go through a gate and continue beside a meadow to cross your last stile to Wanchard Lane.

⑦ Turn left to walk down to the A352 and turn right along the pavement. Turn right again up West Hill to the pub.

PLACES OF INTEREST NEARBY

Wolfeton House, to the south of Charminster, is a fine medieval and Elizabethan house. The massive towers of the gatehouse date from 1500. Open from mid-July to mid-September on Mondays, Wednesdays and Thursdays, 2 pm to 6 pm. Groups by appointment throughout the year. Telephone: 01305 263500.

Cerne Abbas

FROM A RUINED ABBEY TO GIANT HILL

The New Inn

MAP: OS EXPLORER 117 (GR 664014) | **WALK 12** | **DISTANCE:** 3 MILES

DIRECTIONS TO START: CERNE ABBAS IS ABOUT 5 MILES NORTH OF DORCHESTER SIGNED OFF THE A352. **PARKING:** THIS WALK BEGINS FROM A PUBLIC CAR PARK AND PICNIC PLACE. TURN OFF THE A352 DOWN THE LANE SIGNED 'PICNIC PLACE' LEAVING THE VIEWING AREA FOR THE CERNE ABBAS GIANT DIRECTLY ON YOUR LEFT. AFTER ABOUT 50 YARDS TURN LEFT AND PARK.

Find time to explore Cerne Abbas. A historic and beautiful village, it lies cradled in the downs where a little stream finishes its journey south and meets the Cerne. The chalk outline of its famous giant dominates the village from a westward-facing hillside. No two of the fascinating houses lining its narrow streets are alike. Some, half-timbered, project upper storeys over your head, others are stone-built and banded with flint while others reflect the grace of Georgian days with rounded bow windows and pedimented doorways. A Benedictine abbey was founded here in 987. Our walk passes the ruins of the abbey and climbs Giant Hill giving splendid views over the Cerne valley. A gentle descent down the opposite side of the hill brings us back to the village.

The New Inn

This stone-built hostelry has welcomed walkers since the 13th century when it served as a dormitory for the abbey, offering rest and refreshment for passing pilgrims. In the mid-16th century it became Cerne's principal coaching inn. Today the inn continues to offer a warm welcome, well-appointed accommodation and excellent food and drink. The bar areas are spacious and comfortable and there is a separate non-smoking restaurant. Real ales always on tap are brewed by Eldridge Pope. Hardy Country is available and '3 Valley's Ale' which is brewed specially for the New Inn. When we called the guest ale was Courage Directors. There is an extensive, well-chosen wine list.

The menu both in the bar and restaurant offers a wide selection of interesting and varied dishes, for example a breaded sea food platter with scampi, scallops, plaice and cod, a lamb, lemon and mint casserole, rabbit cooked in cider and chicken breast stuffed with Stilton.

In summer the inn is open every day 11 am to 11 pm. In winter, Monday to Saturday 11 am to 2.30 pm and 6 pm to 11 pm; Sundays 12 noon to 2.30 pm and 6 pm to 10.30 pm. Food is served 12 noon to 2 pm and 6 pm to 9 pm.

Behind the inn you will find a patio and a beautiful walled garden with a children's play area. If you fancy a longer stay the New Inn offers excellent accommodation. Telephone: 01300 341274.

The Walk

① Turn left from the entrance to the picnic area to walk down to a stream. Turn

right before the bridge and follow the streamside to a bridge on the left. Cross this and follow the path to Abbey Street. Facing the street on your left is Abbey Farm and the entrance to the abbey ruins.

② With the entrance to the ruins on your left go through an iron gate into the churchyard. Take the left-hand of the two paths ahead to leave the churchyard through another gate. Bear half-right up the meadow which is ridged with embankments. When you reach a dip in the highest embankment and the trees are close on your left, look carefully for a stile a little uphill on the left.

③ Cross the stile and turn left along the foot of Giant Hill. When the path divides take the right-hand path uphill which bears left to the open hillside. Go past the area around the giant to climb the hillside. The soft turf is starred with wild flowers and alive with butterflies in summer.

④ At the top cross a stile into a field. Keep ahead over the field towards the tin roof of a barn.

The mill pond in Cerne Abbas

⑤ When you reach a signpost in front of the barn turn right and walk straight ahead across a field making for a large bush at the far side (there may be no clear path).

⑥ Go through a gate and turn right along the crest of the hill. Below you Cerne Abbas nestles in the valley.

⑦ After about 100 yards you come to a signpost. Navigate carefully here! Ignore the obvious track leading ahead and bear a little left to follow a path downhill towards Cerne Abbas. When you are nearly in the valley the path divides and a narrow path leads right to continue round the foot of Giant Hill. Continue past this turning for about 30 yards and look carefully for another narrow path on the right leading to a stile.

⑧ Turn right over the stile and bear half-left down the meadow to cross a stile on the corner of a sports field. Keep ahead, fence on the left, then turn right along the foot of the meadow to go through a gate on your left to a lane. Turn right into Cerne Abbas. Keep straight on to the New Inn on your left.

To return to your car turn right from the entrance to the New Inn. Turn left up Abbey Street past the church on your right. Note the stocks! Turn left again before Abbey Farm and retrace your steps to the picnic area.

PLACES OF INTEREST NEARBY

The Guest House and **Porch** to the Abbot's lodging can be visited for a small fee.

Minterne Magna Gardens (at their best in spring) are 2 miles north of Cerne Abbas. Open end of March to mid-November, 10 am to 7 pm.

Buckland Newton

PANORAMIC VIEWS OVER THE VALE OF BLACKMOOR

The Gaggle of Geese

MAP: OS EXPLORER 117 (GR 689050)	**WALK 13**	DISTANCE: 3 MILES

DIRECTIONS TO START: BUCKLAND NEWTON IS JUST OFF THE B3143 MIDWAY BETWEEN DORCHESTER AND SHERBORNE. TURN FOR BUCKLAND NEWTON OFF THE B3143, DRIVE PAST THE TURNING INTO CRANES MEADOW AND TAKE THE NEXT LANE ON THE LEFT SIGNED FOR THE PUB. CONTINUE FOR ABOUT ¼ MILE TO THE PUB WHICH IS ON YOUR LEFT. **PARKING:** IN THE PUB CAR PARK.

This is a wonderful walk with a pub to match but make certain you choose a clear day as the views are really breathtaking. Buckland Newton has everything a self-respecting village should have: charming thatched houses and cottages, an ancient church, a fine manor house, a thriving school and, of course, a welcoming pub. Add to these a beautiful setting on the southern fringes of the Blackmoor Vale overlooked by gently rounded hills and you have a walk to remember! Our route follows lanes and meadow paths leading gradually to a splendid ridgeway from where you will enjoy some of Dorset's finest scenery before returning to the pub.

The Gaggle of Geese

Tucked away in the lanes among lush meadowland, this friendly pub is a real 'find'. An impressive whitewashed house, it was built in 1824 and served as the village shop. When it became a pub it was named the Royal Oak, so how did it become the Gaggle of Geese? All was explained to me by the present owner. Evidently the previous landlord kept geese and customers enjoyed seeing the 'gaggle'. The geese still flourish to such an extent that auctions of rare poultry are held in May and September each year, raising thousands of pounds for various local charities. Inside the cool, comfortable bar area images of geese can be spotted everywhere – on the copper hood over the fireplace, on pictures and trays, even vases! The separate restaurant has a charming cottage-like feel with floral print curtains framing casement windows.

Real ales are Badger Best, Ringwood Fortyniner and Ringwood Best and there are always guest ales. Cider is Blackthorn. The emphasis is on good, home-cooked food using local produce and the pub is famous for its steaks. Another popular dish is the 'Pub Classic' composed of ham, fried eggs, baked beans and chips or sausages. A wide range of other bar meals is available or you can choose from the set menu.

Opening times are 12 noon to 2.30 pm and 6.30 pm to 11 pm. Meals are served from 12 noon to 2 pm and 6.30 pm to 10 pm. The pub is deservedly popular so if you intend a group visit let the owners know beforehand so that your meal can be ready for you when you return from your walk. Telephone: 01300 345249 and 345157.

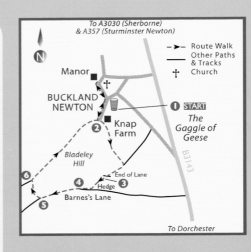

The Walk

① Turn left from the pub car park to walk up the road leaving the pub on your left. Just past the telephone box turn left again along the lane signed 'No Through Road'. After about ¼ mile you pass Knap Farm and a narrow joining lane on the right which is our return route.

② Continue up the concrete lane with views over valleys and woods on your right. After passing a large farm building the way becomes a grassy track and leads through a gate. Walk up the side of the meadow ahead with a hedge close on your left. The meadow dips to a gate. Go through the gate to a stony track. Turn right to follow this path to bring you up to another gate opening to a meadow.

③ There is no clear path at this point and the angle of the blue bridleway arrow is misleading. So you need to navigate carefully! Bearing very slightly right, walk up the meadow to the hedge on the other side. At the hedge, bear right with the hedge on your left, to an iron gate.

Descending Bladeley Hill to Buckland Newton

④ Go through the gate to a track and turn right. This is Barnes's Lane, named after an ancestor of Dorset's famous poet William Barnes. Follow the track for about ½ mile to a grassy, hedged path on the right (no gate).

⑤ Turn right to follow this lovely way between banks colourful with wild flowers in summer, to a crossing path by a large barn.

⑥ Turn right again to follow a ridge path along the crest of Bladeley Hill. It seems as if the whole of the Vale of Blackmoor lies at your feet! Gradually the path descends to meet our earlier route by Knap Farm. Turn left to retrace your steps down the lane and turn right at the end for the pub. To see the church of the Holy Rood, which is full of interest, turn left at the end and walk up the lane which curves right past some attractive cottages. The church stands opposite the imposing manor house. Among the church's many delightful features is a little winding stair leading to a Priest's Room above the south porch, formerly used by the monks of Glastonbury when visiting the parish. Retrace your steps down the lane to return to the Gaggle of Geese.

PLACES OF INTEREST NEARBY

From Buckland Newton it is an easy drive north to **Sherborne** with its splendid abbey and two castles, or south to **Dorchester**, the historic county town.

Stourton Caundle

A TRANQUIL CORNER OF THE BLACKMOOR VALE

The Trooper Inn

MAP: OS EXPLORER 129 (GR 715149)	WALK 14	DISTANCE: 3½ MILES

DIRECTIONS TO START: STOURTON CAUNDLE IS A SMALL VILLAGE IN THE NORTH OF THE BLACKMOOR VALE ABOUT 4 MILES EAST OF SHERBORNE. THE BEST APPROACH IS VIA THE A357 WINCANTON-STURMINSTER ROAD. FOLLOW THE SIGN FOR THE VILLAGE ALONG WATERLOO LANE AND AFTER ABOUT ¾ MILE TURN LEFT. THE LANE CURVES RIGHT TO RUN INTO THE VILLAGE AND THE TROOPER INN IS ON YOUR RIGHT. **PARKING:** IN THE PUB CAR PARK OPPOSITE THE TROOPER OR BEHIND THE PUB.

Stourton Caundle is the most remote of the three Caundle villages close to the border with Somerset. It is a charming place surrounded by a lush countryside of thickly hedged fields and low rounded hills. The church, houses, farms and barns are all built of warm brown stone and a stream winds its way down the village street. It is named after the Stourton family who had a castle here in the 15th century but only the chapel, now used as a barn, and a series of small lakes, originally fishponds, remain. Our walk follows the lanes and bridleways around the village giving wide views over the beautiful Blackmoor Vale.

The Trooper Inn

Here is an inn that Thomas Hardy would have loved! Step through the porch into one of the small low-ceilinged bars either side of the door and you enter another world – the Dorset of a hundred years ago with ancient wooden settles and carved oak tables. Every nook and cranny is hung with a wealth of country bygones collected by the genial landlord, a shepherd for 40 years. And that is not all. Behind the pub a separate building houses the skittle alley and a stunning museum of shepherding memorabilia including three original shepherd's huts and no fewer than 80 melodious sheep bells.

Over 300 years old, the pub was called the Catherine Wheel. When Wellington was recruiting his army to fight Napoleon the soldiers met here so the name was changed to the Trooper. Their choice of rendezvous will come as no surprise! Six real ales are on offer. The four always on tap are Champflower, Oakhill, Exmoor Ale and Ringwood Best. Cider is Thatchers and Burrow Hill. A range of bar snacks includes toasted sandwiches, pasties and ploughman's lunches and among the full meals available is a delicious home-made steak and kidney pie.

Opening times are 12 noon to 2 pm (closed at lunchtime on Mondays) and 7 pm to 11 pm (10.30 pm on Sundays). Meals are served every lunchtime except Monday, no meals in the evening.

There is a pleasantly shaded garden and children's play area. The museum and skittle alley which has its own bar can be hired for private functions and from June to August the inn can cater for up to fifty people with Dorset cream teas. Telephone: 01963 362405.

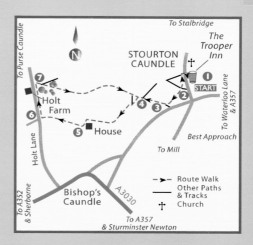

The Walk

① Turn right from the porch of the Trooper. The Manor House on your left was once owned by the much-loved children's author Enid Blyton. Walk up the village street past a chapel and turn left just past a phone box following bridleway and footpath signs. After a few yards ignore the footpath sign ahead and turn left following the blue bridleway sign. Keep straight ahead through a farmyard and go through a gate to walk up a track.

② Disregard a gate and footpath sign a little to your left and go through the gate ahead following the bridleway sign. Now a pleasant path leads you along a ridge with lovely views over the Vale to a gate opening to a stony track.

③ Turn right imediately up the track (not the road a few yards away on your left). After about ¼ mile you will see prominent footpath signs on your right. Continue for about 50 yards then look carefully in the hedge on your left for a footpath sign and stile.

Descending the bridleway to Stourton Caundle from Holt Wood

④ Cross the stile into a field and keep straight ahead over the corner of the field to go through a gate to a track. Turn left along the track which doglegs right then left to go through a gate and run downhill. In the valley the track curves right uphill between barns and swings left past a house on the left (the route differs slightly from the OS map here) to meet an asphalt drive.

⑤ Turn right and follow the drive to Holt Lane.

⑥ Turn right along this quiet lane for about ½ mile. Pass Holt Farm on your left and opposite some buildings about 80 yards further on turn right through a gate along the bridleway signed for Stourton Caundle.

⑦ The bridleway leads through woods to a division. Take the right-hand path and continue through the woods to cross a stile into an open field. Keep ahead beside the field, hedge on the right. The path becomes a wide way, running along a ridge with splendid views. Bordered at first with oak trees it plunges through a deep hollow then continues between hedges past some farm buildings on the right. The way becomes stony and passes the stile we climbed outbound at point 4. Retrace your steps as you continue down the track, turning left just before you come to the road to follow the bridleway through the farmyard, turning right then right again to return to the Trooper.

PLACES OF INTEREST NEARBY
Purse Caundle Manor, to the north-west – a beautiful Elizabethan house. Open May to September, Thursday and Sunday 2 pm to 5 pm and Bank Holiday Mondays. Telephone: 01963 250400.

Ansty

A MEANDER BY THE DEVIL'S BROOK

The Fox Inn

MAP: OS EXPLORER 117 (GR 767033)   **WALK 15**   **DISTANCE:** 2¼ MILES

DIRECTIONS TO START: THE BEST APPROACH IS VIA THE A354 BLANDFORD FORUM-DORCHESTER ROAD. LEAVE THE A354 IN MILBORNE ST ANDREW HEADING NORTH, SIGNED FOR ANSTY AND MILTON ABBAS (THERE IS A BROWN SIGN FOR THE FOX INN ALSO). CONTINUE FOR 2 MILES THEN TURN LEFT FOR ANSTY. AFTER ABOUT 4 MILES TURN LEFT AGAIN AT ANSTY CROSS, SIGNED FOR MELCOMBE BINGHAM. THE FOX INN IS ABOUT ½ MILE DOWN THE LANE, IN LOWER ANSTY. **PARKING:** PATRONS MAY LEAVE CARS IN THE INN CAR PARK. ALTERNATIVELY PARK IN THE VICINITY OF THE VILLAGE HALL, JUST SOUTH OF THE FOX.

The Dorset downs shelter many secrets and this walk takes you to one of the county's least known and most remote places, the valley of the Devil's Brook. This little stream, whose name fortunately only means 'dark', rises in the downs near Ansty where we begin our walk. From the village, field paths with wide views over the valley lead to Bingham's Melcombe, a late medieval manor in glorious surroundings. Meadow paths beside the Devil's Brook lead us back to Ansty and the Fox Inn.

The Fox Inn

The Fox Inn is deservedly popular, offering a warm welcome to everyone. It has all the charm of a country house hotel but those of us who arrive with rucksacks and muddy boots have no need to worry. At the entrance to the comfortable Ansty Bar a large notice says 'Walkers Welcome!' Inside, the relaxed family atmosphere is a reminder that this 200 year old inn was once the home of Charles Hall who founded a brewery here in 1777. He adopted his niece who married Edward Woodhouse. Hall and Woodhouse brewery has since moved to Blandford Forum and in 1915 the family home became the Fox Inn.

Real ales include Tanglefoot and Badger Best, cider is Blackthorn and there is an extensive wine list. All the food is home-cooked, specialising in local produce. In the Ansty Bar you can sample a wide range of snacks and choose from a comprehensive menu. Delicious steak and ale pies and mixed grills are always popular and lighter meals include Wessex pasties and baked potato skins filled with tuna and cheese. A carvery is served in the lounge bar and à la carte dishes in the Woodhouse restaurant.

Children and dogs are welcome and there is a large garden. Opening times are 11 am to 11 pm every day all the week. Meals are served 11 am to 3 pm and 7 pm to 10 pm. Accommodation includes 14 well-appointed bedrooms and a bunkhouse with all facilities. Telephone: 01258 880328.

The Walk

① Turn left from the front of the Fox and walk down the road past the Old Brewery building, now the village hall. Cross the Devil's Brook, called at this point Mash Water as it was once the drain from the brewery. Follow the road past a footpath sign on the left (our return route) and continue through part of Melcombe Bingham. The road rises to a cluster of thatched cottages.

② Take the track on the left opposite Forge Cottage (the sign for Bingham's Melcombe is hard to spot). Go through a gate and follow the narrow path ahead over a large field. Continue past a finger of woodland on your right along the edge of a field. As the path begins to curve left look for some wooden bars a little to your right. Cross these, walk through the trees and keep straight on over the next field. Ahead you will see Bingham's Melcombe manor house cradled in the valley. Keep ahead over the grass to cross a stile to the smooth green lawn beside the walls of the manor garden.

③ Turn right to a gravel track and bear left to follow the track past the manor

The great yew hedge at Bingham's Melcombe

gatehouse on the left and the church and little school on the right. The school was built in memory of Caroline Damer Bingham and inscribed 'Feed my lambs'. The manor was the home of the Bingham family for over six hundred years, and once there was a village in this enchanted valley. Cross the footbridge beside the lake and go round the barrier.

④ Turn left close to the fence on your left and keep ahead to cross the stile beside a gate. Bear a little left round the meadow keeping the trees close on your left. The path may not be clear but keep the boundary fence on your left and look for a stile ahead. Cross the stile and follow the path over a dip with a fence on your left and trees on your right. Cross the next stile into a meadow. Keeping the fence a few yards away on your left continue over the meadow for about 100 yards then go through a gap on your left. The path bears half-right over a narrow meadow.

⑤ Cross the stiles and footbridge and walk up to a well-defined crossing path.

⑥ Bear right uphill past a joining path on the left and at the top cross a stile into a field. Continue with a wood on your right. After a gate the path descends the meadow to run close to the Devil's Brook which is on your right. Keep straight ahead crossing several stiles and ignoring all tracks leading over the brook. A final stile brings you to the lane where we began our walk. Turn right to return to the Fox.

PLACES OF INTEREST NEARBY
Milton Abbey and **Milton Abbas**, 4 miles east of Ansty. For details see Walk 22.

West Knighton

THROUGH THE WATER MEADOWS OF THE FROME VALLEY

The New Inn

MAP: OS OUTDOOR LEISURE 15 (GR 733879) | **WALK 16** | **DISTANCE:** 2½ MILES

DIRECTIONS TO START: WEST KNIGHTON VILLAGE IS SIGNED IN BROADMAYNE OFF THE A352 DORCHESTER-WAREHAM ROAD. FOLLOW THE ROAD ROUND TO THE RIGHT TO PASS THE VILLAGE CHURCH. THE ROAD CURVES LEFT TO THE NEW INN. **PARKING:** THE NEW INN CAR PARK.

As you follow the route of this walk through the beautiful wooded countryside on the southern fringes of the Frome valley you will feel you are stepping back in time and entering the world of Thomas Hardy. From a picturesque old-world village, field paths lead to a forgotten valley hidden in oak woods. We return through the meadows with views over gently undulating countryside. Find time to visit West Knighton church, sensitively restored in 1893 from sketches made by Thomas Hardy.

The New Inn

There is nothing new about this attractive inn, its old walls thickly clothed with ivy and roof edged, in true Dorset style, with stone slabs. Some time in the distant past it was a row of farm cottages and probably became a pub around 200 years ago. Inside you will find a warm welcome. Once, I am assured by a reputable authority, you would also have found a magical 'yes/no' table. Sit at the table and wish and your wish came true! Unfortunately it fell to pieces when the landlord who owned it left. To the right of the bar is a delightful secluded restaurant known as 'The Gallery'. The walls are hung with a selection of fine paintings of country scenes, the work of a local artist. Most are for sale.

The food is well prepared and attractively presented. When we called a wide range of bar meals included ploughman's with ham and pineapple and Stilton and apple. Among the 'specials' were braised beef in Guinness and a tasty chicken korma. Interesting 'afters' included Stilton with black grapes. Real ales are Ringwood Best and Old Thumper and there are guest ales such as Worthington and Ushers Best.

Monday to Friday opening hours are 12 noon to 2.30 pm and 6.30 pm to 11 pm. Weekends the inn is open 12 noon to 2.45 pm and 6.30 pm to 11 pm (Sunday evenings 7.30 pm to 10.30 pm). Meals are served 12 noon to 2 pm and 6.30 pm to 9 pm. There is an attractive garden and a safe play area for children. Telephone: 01305 852349.

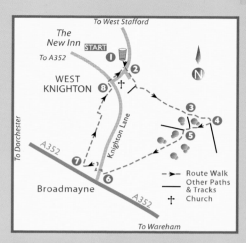

The Walk

① Leaving the front of the New Inn on your left turn right up the road past thatched houses and cottages, some dating from the 17th century. On the left you pass the former village school with its school house, dated 1865.

② As the road curves right, turn left up the lane, Hardy's Row. For the first part of our walk we follow the sign for the Jubilee Trail, a white arrow on a green background. The lane becomes a gravel track leading through a small wooden gate past a very pretty row of cottages and a metal barrier. Turn left up a narrow path and bear right for a few yards to footpath signs. Take the footpath on the left to cross a stile. Walk over the field bearing very slightly right to go over double stiles. Continue over fields and stiles towards woodland.

③ When you reach the trees cross double stiles. Bear left along the foot of the field with trees on your right. Cross a stile and keep ahead to go over another stile. Continue for about 50 yards until you come to a wooden footbridge on the right.

Thatched cottages in West Knighton village

Broadmayne. After going through a gate the path narrows and bears a little right through another gate to Knighton Lane.

⑥ Turn right for about 100 yards, then take the footpath on the left, signed 'To the Church'. The path runs beside a wall on the right and over a stile. Bear left to go through a small wooden gate into the new churchyard. Pass part of the old churchyard on your left and bear right in front of a wall through a gate to a footpath sign for West Knighton.

⑦ Turn right to walk down the meadow. Cross double stiles and keep ahead up the field to a crossing track in front of a hedge. Turn left for about 40 yards then cross the stile on the right to continue over a field in the direction of West Knighton.

⑧ When you reach Knighton Lane turn left then follow the road as it curves right past the church. Bear left past Hardy's Row to retrace your steps to the New Inn.

④ Turn right over the bridge and with Watergates Cottage close on your right follow the track through the trees to a Y-junction. Here we leave the Jubilee Trail. Turn right and follow the track past a joining track on the right. About 50 yards further, opposite a row of cottages, look carefully for a narrow footpath signed on the left leading through woodland.

⑤ Turn left and follow the narrow path through the trees. Bear slightly right through an iron swing gate. A lovely meadow path now leads ahead to take you through another swing gate. Continue along the path with a fence on your left at first then keep to the path beside a field. Go through a gate and continue along a raised path towards the houses of

PLACES OF INTEREST NEARBY

Kingston Maurward Park, just east of Dorchester off the A35 – splendid animals and gardens. Open daily 1 pm to 5 pm, Easter to mid-October. Telephone: 01305 264738.

Max Gate, Thomas Hardy's Dorchester home. Open 2 pm to 5 pm Sunday, Monday and Wednesday from April to September. Telephone: 01305 262538. **Thomas Hardy's Birthplace**, Higher Bockhampton, north-east of Dorchester. Open from April to October, 11 am to 5 pm except Friday and Saturday. Telephone: 01305 262366.

Osmington Mills

STROLLING BY WEYMOUTH'S DRAMATIC COASTLINE

The Smugglers' Inn

MAP: OS OUTDOOR LEISURE 15 (GR 737818)   **WALK 17**   **DISTANCE:** 3 MILES

DIRECTIONS TO START: OSMINGTON MILLS IS ABOUT 5 MILES EAST OF WEYMOUTH. TURN FOR OSMINGTON MILLS OFF THE A353 AND CONTINUE FOR ABOUT ¾ MILE. THE SMUGGLERS' INN IS AT THE FOOT OF THE HILLSIDE ON YOUR LEFT AND THE CAR PARK IS SIGNED OFF THE ROAD ON YOUR RIGHT. **PARKING:** IN THE INN CAR PARK. ASK PERMISSION BEFORE LEAVING YOUR CAR FOR THE WALK.

A smugglers' cove, a spectacular stretch of the Dorset Coast Path and one of the county's prettiest villages must surely make this walk a favourite with all the family. You could be misled by the name of our starting point! Here you will find no signs of industry, just a small hamlet tucked in a steep ravine opening to the sea with a magnificent view over Portland Harbour and Weymouth Bay. Our route along the coast path affords more splendid sea views and runs through richly varied scenery. We turn inland to visit Osmington village. One of our most loved landscape painters, John Constable, spent his honeymoon here in 1816 and made a number of sketches and paintings of its charming stone-built, dark-thatched houses. Meadow paths lead back to the Smugglers' Inn.

The Smugglers' Inn

The 'Smuggs', as this fine old inn is called by locals, has welcomed travellers since the 13th century. Sandwiched between sheer cliffs at the foot of the ravine, it provided a convenient landing place for smugglers during the 18th and early 19th century. Boats with contraband cargoes of brandy, silks and tobacco would be drawn silently onto the beach close by under the watchful eyes of look-outs posted on the headlands. The inn was the headquarters of a particularly notorious smuggler, Pierre Latour. With its low ceilings crossed by massive black beams, huge fireplaces and secret alcoves the inn is still full of the atmosphere of those days and it would come as no surprise to see 'French Peter', as he was called in the trade, plotting the next run over a foaming jug of ale!

Today everyone is made welcome and there is a special room for families. Real ales include Badger Best and Tanglefoot. The guest ale when we called was Fursty Ferret. Seafood is a speciality and the inn is famous for lobster. Examples of the wide range of dishes are 'Lamb Boulangère' served in a red wine and herb sauce, chicken, Stilton and bacon pie and, in summer, a choice of salads.

During the summer the inn is open 11 am to 11 pm and food is served all day. At other times opening hours are 11 am to 2.30 pm and 6.30 pm to 11 pm with meals served from 12 noon to 2 pm and 6 pm to 9 pm. On fine days you can enjoy sitting by the stream in the garden and there is a safe play area for children. Dogs on leads are welcome in the garden. Excellent overnight accommodation is also available. Telephone: 01305 833125.

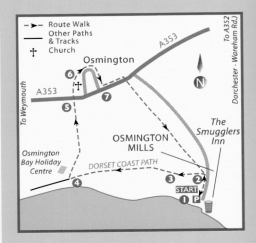

The Walk

① Return to the road and turn left following the sign 'Coast Path Weymouth and Osmington'. Continue up the road for about 300 yards and as the road curves right, turn left along the signed footpath. The narrow path runs uphill to another sign.

② Turn left, 'Coast Path Weymouth', and follow the path rising gently uphill. Almost at the top you come to a stile on your left.

③ Cross the stile then bear right with a fence close on your right. Now you stand high on the grassy clifftop and ahead you look down on another world of wooded clefts and tiny streams.

The path descends to a stile on the left. Cross this and follow the sign through the tangled glades of the landslips over boardwalks, bridges and stiles. The path leads up steps to bring you to open grassland once more. Continue along the hillside over two stiles and follow the path as it descends to a stile facing Osmington Bay Holiday Centre.

The view from the Coast Path near Osmington Mills

④ Do not cross the stile but turn right up the meadow to a stile on your left. Cross this to a lane and bear right up the lane past the Holiday Centre on your left to meet the A353.

⑤ Cross the road, go over a stile and follow the footpath over another stile to walk beside a field with a hedge on your right. After about 100 yards turn right over a stile and go through a gate into the churchyard in Osmington. Pass the church on your right and the ruins of the former manor house of the Warham family – now set in a beautiful private garden – on your left and leave the churchyard by the lychgate.

⑥ Turn left, then just past the post office bear right along the village street. Turn right again along Chapel Lane and continue to rejoin the A353.

⑦ Turn left beside the road. Pass Craigs Dairy Farm on the right and about 50 yards further on bear right following the sign for Osmington Mills. Cross a bridge and stile and continue up the meadow ahead to another stile. The path bears slightly left to the next stile which you cross to a signpost. Our way bears a little right down the meadow. Over the next stile the path leads beside a field, hedge on the left, to bring you over a final stile to meet our earlier route at point 2. Retrace your steps, turning right down the road to the Smugglers' Inn.

PLACES OF INTEREST NEARBY

Lodmoor Nature Reserve, a few miles west of Osmington. An acre of wetland north of the **Sea Life Country Park**. A prolific bird-breeding ground with footpaths and observation hides. Telephone: 01305 788255.

Tolpuddle

WHERE HISTORY WAS MADE

The Martyrs' Inn

MAP: OS EXPLORER 117 (GR 795945)	**WALK 18**	DISTANCE: 3 MILES

DIRECTIONS TO START: TOLPUDDLE IS NOW BYPASSED BY THE A35 BETWEEN DORCHESTER AND BERE REGIS. LEAVE THE A35 FOLLOWING SIGNS FOR THE VILLAGE. THE MARTYRS' INN FACES THE ROAD. **PARKING:** IN THE MARTYRS' INN CAR PARKS ON EITHER SIDE OF THE BUILDING.

Tolpuddle must be the most famous village in Dorset! Even without the momentous events that took place there in the 1830s it would be an attractive place to visit with its beautiful valley setting, historic church and rows of cob and thatch cottages. But the village owes its world-wide fame to six farm labourers who, faced with a reduction in their pitiful wage of nine shillings a week, banded together to form a Trade Union. This was not illegal but in order to strengthen their position, new members took an oath of secrecy. For this they were arrested in 1834 and transported to Botany Bay. The outrage inflamed public opinion and after two years they were pardoned and returned to England.

You will discover more of their story as you follow this walk in the countryside they knew, the Piddle (or Puddle!) valley.

The Martyrs' Inn

Since the building of the bypass this comfortable and welcoming inn has returned to being the centre of village life. An inn has stood on the site beside the Dorchester highway for over 350 years and served as a staging post for goods between Poole, Salisbury and Blandford. An earlier hostelry was built so close to the road that its sign was repeatedly knocked down by passing coaches! Appropriately named to commemorate the six early Trade Unionists whose sufferings earned them the name of martyrs, there are many reminders of them in the spacious bar area and separate restaurant.

You will eat and drink well at the Martyrs. Real ales are Badger Best, Champion and Tanglefoot and there is an extensive wine list. Tempting meals on offer range from baguettes with a variety of fillings including bacon and mushrooms and home-cooked ham and salad, to such dishes as breast of duck in bacon and lentil sauce and cod and prawn in cayenne and cheese sauce. They are never too busy at the Martyrs to put the kettle on if you fancy a cup of tea and – a real bonus for walkers! – they serve a substantial breakfast.

The inn is open all day 11 am to 12 pm and food is available 11 am to 2.30 pm and 6.30 pm to 9.30 pm except on Sunday evenings. Telephone: 01305 848249.

The Walk

① Leave the front porch of the inn and turn right to walk through the village. In front of the green the road divides. Take the

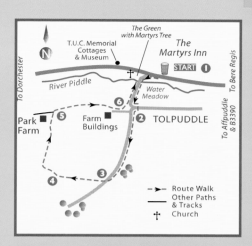

left-hand lane. On the green on the right the Martyrs' seat and shelter stand beside the sycamore where it is said the six labourers met to make their plans. Follow the lane as it leads past the manor house and the mill to cross the river and the water meadows. Formerly the meadows were used for grazing sheep and date from 1630. They were laid down on the warm water of chalk springs which, controlled by hatches, encouraged the growth of early grass. The lane curves left past a bridleway sign on the right and shortly after divides.

② Take the right-hand lane and follow it, past a joining track on the right, for about ³/₄ mile. After passing a wood on the left lower hedges reveal a view over meadows towards woodland ahead. Look carefully for an iron farm gate on the right with a half-hidden stile beside it.

③ Turn right through the gate and follow the wide grassy track beside fields with a hedge on your right. Continue for a little over ¹/₄ mile to pass a farm gate on your right. About 100 yards further on the path leads to another iron farm gate.

The sycamore and memorial seat on the green where the Martyrs met

⑤ Turn right and follow the lane along the valley. The tiny Piddle flows through the meadows on your left. Just past some farm buildings our path leaves the lane and bears a little left to cross a narrow field. Go through a wooden gate and bear left to the lane we followed earlier in our walk.

⑥ Retrace your steps down the lane to cross the river. Turn right in the village for the Martyrs Inn. Before returning to the inn you may like to turn left to see the church and visit the Memorial Cottages.

PLACES OF INTEREST NEARBY

The TUC Memorial Cottages were built in 1934 in memory of the Tolpuddle Martyrs. A central hallway houses a museum. Each year on 'Martyrs' Day', the third Sunday in July, it is the scene of a gathering of over 5,000 people! Open April to October, 10 am to 5.30 pm except Mondays. Shorter hours in winter. Telephone: 01305 848237.

Athelhampton House, 2 miles west of the village, is a magnificent house dating from 1485, with outstanding gardens. Open March to October daily (except Saturdays) 10.30 am to 5 pm; November to February, Sundays 10.30 am to dusk. Telephone: 01305 848363.

④ Bear very slightly right through the gate to follow a beautiful grassy path between banks of summertime flowers and low hedges which curves right to wind its way down to the valley floor. Go through a gate to leave Park Farm on your left and meet a lane.

Lulworth Cove

A DORSET GEM

The Lulworth Cove Hotel

MAP: OS OUTDOOR LEISURE 15 (GR 822802)   **WALK 19**   **DISTANCE:** 1¾ MILES

DIRECTIONS TO START: THE BEST APPROACH TO LULWORTH COVE IS OFF THE A352 WAREHAM-DORCHESTER ROAD. LEAVE THE A352 AT WOOL AND FOLLOW THE SIGNS FOR WEST LULWORTH ALONG THE B3071. WHEN THIS ROAD TURNS FOR EAST LULWORTH KEEP STRAIGHT ON ALONG THE B3070 TO DRIVE THROUGH WEST LULWORTH. TURN RIGHT INTO THE PUBLIC CAR PARK AT THE APPROACH TO THE COVE. **PARKING:** THE CAR PARK IS BEHIND THE HERITAGE CENTRE OPPOSITE THE LULWORTH COVE HOTEL.

Lulworth Cove, a perfect bay shaped like a scallop shell between sheer limestone cliffs, is one of the most thrilling places to visit on the Dorset coast. In spite of its popularity, the village which clusters around the road to the Cove retains its charm with many stone-built thatched houses and a mill pond surrounded by summertime flowers. From the village we take a cliff path to look down into Stair Hole, a tide-filled chasm among rocks contorted by a collision between European and African land masses about 15 million years ago. We then climb a woodland path to the grassy slopes of Bindon Hill. A beautiful ridge walk along the crest of Bindon Hill leads us to West Lulworth before we take a lower path to our starting point near the Lulworth Cove Hotel.

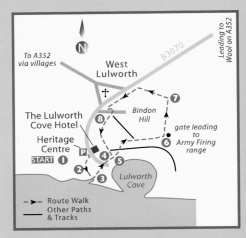

The Lulworth Cove Hotel

This attractive inn was once the manor house, dating back 400 years. In earlier times hotel guests would alight at the coach house which until recently stood on the opposite side of the road. It is ideal for walkers, spacious and comfortable with blazing log fires in winter. In the bar or separate restaurant you can choose from a tempting array of dishes which include locally caught lobster and crabs and 'Cove Seafood Platter' served with lemon and dips. Examples of the meat dishes are 'Pork Steak Normandie' grilled and flavoured with a cider sauce and 'Chicken Asparagus' served in wine and cream. Real ales are from Burton and Tetley, the cider is Blackthorn and there is an extensive wine list. The pleasant garden is screened from the road.

Opening times in summer are 11 am to 11 pm and at other times of the year 11.30 am to 2.30 pm and 7 pm to 9.30 pm. Meals are served 12 noon to 2.30 pm and 7 pm to 9.30 pm. The hotel offers excellent accommodation. A bonus for walkers is a leaflet with details of other walks in this lovely area. Telephone: 01929 400333.

The Walk

NB: Allow plenty of time as the route includes two fairly steep but short climbs.

① Return to the road from the car park and turn right past the Heritage Centre following the sign for Stair Hole.

② Pass the Coastguard Station on your right then just past a joining track on the left turn left along a track indicated by a green arrow. This leads along the clifftop giving magnificent views over Lulworth Cove and Stair Hole. Follow the cliff path to the telescope mounted on the look-out point.

③ With your back to the telescope walk down the grass ahead towards a red mine case. Pass the mine case on your right and descend the steps to the road.

④ Cross the road and climb the steps to the left of the Beach Café. The path climbs quite steeply up the wooded hillside but steps at intervals make the going easier. Cross a stile to emerge on the open slopes of Bindon Hill.

⑤ Navigate carefully here! We have no clear path at this point. Ignore the signs for paths to left and right and bear half-right up the hillside to a crossing path. Go over this and take the narrow path ahead which winds a little left round the hillside then bears right to become a broad green way heading east along the crest of Bindon Hill. You cross a dyke believed to have been erected in the 5th century BC by Iron Age

Lulworth Cove

mmigrants and come to one of the entrance gates for the Army Range walks (the route differs slightly from OS map).

⑥ Do not go through the gate but turn left and descend the hill. Go over a stile, cross a track and continue downhill to a stile on your left.

⑦ Turn left over the stile and follow a pleasant terraced path overlooking the rooftops of West Lulworth on your right. Disregard all joining paths on the right. The path becomes a lane (Sunnyside) and leads to a wide track. Turn left for about 30 yards to a stile at the foot of Bindon Hill on your right.

⑧ Turn right over the stile, ignore the sign for the Youth Hostel and follow the path leading gently uphill with a hedge close on your right. The path traces the

hillside to bring you back to the stile we crossed earlier in the walk at point 5. Turn right over the stile and retrace your steps to the Cove. Bear right up the road to the Lulworth Cove Hotel and the car park.

PLACES OF INTEREST NEARBY

Lulworth Cove Heritage Centre – open every day, 1st March to 1st November 10 am to 6 pm, rest of the year 10 am to 4 pm. Telephone: 01929 400587.

Lulworth Castle, East Lulworth. Historic home of the Weld family. Open every day 1st April to 1st November 10 am to 6 pm, rest of the year 10 am to 4 pm. Telephone: 01929 400510.

The Doll's House, Lulworth Cove. Timber-framed fisherman's cottage dating from 1840. Opening times vary. Telephone: 01929 400165.

Winterborne Whitechurch

A WALK IN A SECRET VALLEY

The Milton Arms

MAP: OS EXPLORER 117 (GR 838002)   **WALK 20**   **DISTANCE:** 3 MILES

DIRECTIONS TO START: WINTERBORNE WHITECHURCH IS ABOUT 7 MILES SOUTH-WEST OF BLANDFORD FORUM BESIDE THE A354. THE MILTON ARMS ADJOINS THE A354 ON THE CORNER OF CHESCOMBE LANE. **PARKING:** IN THE MILTON ARMS CAR PARK IN FRONT OF THE PUB.

The Winterborne valley is Dorset at its most serene and peaceful. There are no crowds, no rush, little traffic, just miles of tranquil footpaths dipping through the downland countryside and leading through woods and meadows rich in wild flowers. This easy stroll takes you into the heart of this bewitching valley. And it will have a special appeal if you love fine trees as part of the route runs through the parkland surrounding Whatcombe House, an 18th century mansion built for the Pleydell family who still retain their long association with the parish.

The Milton Arms

This friendly black and white pub in the oldest part of Winterborne Whitechurch has been a haven for travellers between Dorchester and Blandford Forum since the 17th century. But it has very close links with today especially with the Armed Services. You will see a splendid collection of naval photographs and shields decorating the walls of the lounge bar, including a photograph of a local hero.

Whether you would like a snack, a full meal or just a drink you will enjoy it in comfort at the Milton Arms! Wooden armchairs are drawn up to tables decorated with candles and flowers and there is a separate non-smoking area. Real ales are Flowers Original, Bass and Tetley Mild, cider is Scrumpy Jack and a choice of wines is available. As well as an à la carte menu there is a seasonally varied specials board. When we called these included salmon steak in a mornay sauce, steak pie in Guinness and cider, braised venison faggots and a delicious cheese, onion and mushroom quiche.

Opening times are 11 am to 2.30 pm and 7 pm to 11 pm during the week and on Sunday 12 noon to 3 pm and 7 pm to 10.30 pm. Meals are served 12 noon to 2 pm and 7 pm to 9.30 pm. Telephone: 01258 880306.

The Walk

① Turn left from the car park in front of the pub to walk about 30 yards along Chescombe Lane with your back to the main road. Take the first lane on the right to pass the school and village hall. The lane becomes a concrete track rising gently

between tall hedges. As you gain height lovely views over the Winterborne valley unfold on your right.

② The crossing track here is a right-of-way but the path ahead is signed 'Private'. Turn left over a stile by a gate and follow the wide grassy track towards a barn.

③ Pass the barn on your left and immediately after turn right along a field path with a hedge on your left. The path bears a little left then continues with a wood on your right to a stile by a gate. Go over the stile to a crosstrack.

④ Turn right to walk through a beautiful wood of young beech trees open enough to be carpeted with bluebells in May. The track descends a little to leave the wood and rises to continue through more open countryside between hedges to enter another wood. This is aptly named Cliff Wood as the hillside falls away steeply on your left as you descend to a junction of four paths.

⑤ Turn right and keep ahead along a

The beautiful medieval pulpit in the church at Winterborne Whitechurch

shallow valley with meadows rising on your left and woods at first on your right. Soon you pass more open parkland studded with splendid trees. The path becomes a lane past cottages which brings you to the valley road.

⑥ Bear right beside the road for about 200 yards crossing the Winterborne stream to a track on the left opposite an entrance to Whatcombe House.

⑦ Turn left and continue up the track between two houses to a gate.

⑧ Go through the gate. Now navigate carefully! Ignore the more obvious track leading ahead and turn half-right along a grassy path over the meadow. A gate opens through a hedge to a clear track which leads you slightly uphill to run beside a wood on your right.

⑨ On the corner of the wood, facing a meadow you come to a crosspath. Turn right with the field on your left and keep ahead into the wood. When you come to a crosspath bear right for just a few yards and you will see our path clearly on the left. Bear left to resume your original heading downhill through the wood. The path narrows by a fence. For about 150 yards it may be overgrown but it is passable. Then an open path leads down the field to cross a little plank bridge over the Winterborne and two stiles and bring you back to the valley road.

⑩ Bear left for a few yards then turn right up the track signed for Chescombe. This rises to give you a glimpse of Whatcombe House on your right before it meets our outward bound route at point 2. Turn left to retrace your steps back to Winterborne Whitechurch and the pub. Find time if you can before you leave the village to visit the church. It dates from the 12th century and holds much of interest including a unique medieval pulpit.

PLACES OF INTEREST NEARBY

Milton Abbey, reached along Chescombe Lane to the west, survived the Dissolution of the Monasteries in 1539. This superb church has a magnificent tower and its treasures include a rood-loft with medieval portraits and an oak hanging tabernacle. Close by is the picture-postcard village of **Milton Abbas**, designed by 'Capability' Brown in the 18th century.

Winterborne Stickland

IN THE SHADOW OF BULBARROW
The Shire Horse

MAP: OS EXPLORER 117 (GR 836048)	WALK 21	DISTANCE: 3 MILES

DIRECTIONS TO START: WINTERBORNE STICKLAND IS ABOUT 6 MILES WEST OF BLANDFORD FORUM. THE BEST APPROACH IS VIA THE A354. TURN FOR WINTERBORNE STICKLAND IN WINTERBORNE WHITECHURCH, CONTINUE FOR ABOUT 3 MILES TO THE SHIRE HORSE INN WHICH IS ON YOUR RIGHT. **PARKING:** IN THE SHIRE HORSE CAR PARK.

The Winterborne stream rises in the chalk downs and flows south to meet the Stour. Close to its source it carves a deep valley sheltering one of Dorset's most charming villages, Winterborne Stickland. Whitewashed cob and thatched houses mix happily with newer dwellings and colourful gardens fringe the stream. Our walk climbs gently out of the valley to give glorious views before woodland paths lead to a steep descent through the meadows to the source of the stream at Winterborne Houghton, a pretty village nestling at the foot of the eastern slopes of Bulbarrow. To return you have a choice of routes: an attractive lane or a field path. Both will take you back to our starting point, the Shire Horse inn.

The Shire Horse

The Shire Horse must be everyone's idea of a real village inn with its cob walls, deep thatch and tiny casement windows framed by dark beams. The building dates from the early 1700s and at that time the owners drew their water from the well near the entrance which I am told is over 85 ft deep! Inside there is a comfortable bar area for a drink and snack. More substantial meals can be enjoyed in the separate restaurant. The menu, featuring good home-cooking, includes such dishes as sirloin steak with a white wine and cucumber sauce and beef and Guinness pie. Among the sweets there is a tempting Dorset apple cake. Real ales are London Pride and Bass. The inn has a sheltered courtyard and a terraced garden.

Opening times are from 12 noon to 2.30 pm and 7 pm to 11 pm (Sunday 7 pm to 10.30 pm). Meals are served on Tuesday to Sunday (and on Bank Holiday Mondays) from 12 noon to 2.15 pm (Saturday and Sunday 2.30 pm) and 7 pm to 9.30 pm. Meals are not served on Sunday night in winter. Telephone: 01258 880838.

The Walk

① Turn right from the inn car park passing the pub on your right. After about 150 yards turn left up a gravel path signed for Winterborne Houghton. The path climbs gently between hedges. Cross a stile and follow the path half-left over a field. The path curves right.

② After about 100 yards look carefully for a stile on the left. Cross the stile and follow the narrow path downhill to go over a wooden bridge to a lane.

③ Turn right for about 100 yards then take the footpath on the left leading uphill to a stile. Cross the stile and continue up the wooded hillside. Go over another stile to leave the woods and meet a lane.

④ Bear right for just a few yards then turn left beside Valley View Farm and go through a gate. Follow the gravel track ahead past some farm buildings.

⑤ Ignore the gate on the right and go through the gate immediately ahead. Bear half-right diagonally down the meadow then climb up to the point in the far corner where three hedges converge. Go through a gate and walk up the next meadow with a hedge on your right.

⑥ Go through a gate to a crosspath. Turn right for about 50 yards then keep to the path as it bears left over a field towards woods. The path curves a little right then left to enter the pinewoods of New Coppice. Continue through the wood for

Descending the hillside into Winterborne Houghton

...bout 200 yards to a meeting point of four ...aths. (To see a beautiful beech wood keep ...head for about 50 yards then return to ...oint 7.)

⑦ Our way is right here (left if you have ...ade the detour). Follow the woodland ...ath to a Y-junction.

⑧ Take the right-hand path to leave the ...ood through a gate and keep ahead beside ...field, hedge on the right, to go through ...he next gate to a lane.

⑨ Cross the lane and take the footpath beside a fence on the left which curves right to go through a gate. Keeping a hedge close on your left walk downhill through more gates. The path drops steeply through a gate to a farmyard. Bear a little right and follow the signs leaving the farm buildings on your left to go through a final gate to a gravel track. Descend the track to a Y-junction.

⑩ Take the left-hand path over the cattle grid to walk through beautiful gardens past Winterborne Houghton church to the village street.

⑪ Now you have a choice. You can if you wish turn right here to follow the attractive lane back to Winterborne Stickland. When you reach the village pass the church on your left and turn left for the pub. Or you can return along a field path. Turn left for a few yards then turn right, signed 'Bulbarrow'. After about 100 yards turn right along the footpath, cross a stile and continue parallel with the lane. Just past some farm buildings go through a gate then bear half-right to go through another gate to a grassy track. Turn left and keep ahead following the footpath signs through gates to rejoin our outward bound route by the stile at point 2. Retrace your steps to the pub.

PLACES OF INTEREST NEARBY
Blandford Forum is a splendid Georgian market town and its **Museum** illustrates the community's life and culture. Open between April and late September, Tuesday to Saturday, 10 am to 4 pm. Telephone: 01258 451115.

Hinton St Mary

IN THE FOOTSTEPS OF WILLIAM BARNES

The White Horse Inn

MAP: OS EXPLORER 129 (GR 787162)	WALK 22	DISTANCE: 3 MILES

DIRECTIONS TO START: HINTON ST MARY IS BESIDE THE B3092 A MILE NORTH OF
STURMINSTER NEWTON. APPROACHING FROM STURMINSTER, DRIVE INTO THE VILLAGE
AND TAKE THE FIRST ROAD ON THE RIGHT TO THE WHITE HORSE INN ON YOUR LEFT.
APPROACHING FROM THE NORTH DRIVE INTO THE VILLAGE AND TAKE THE SECOND
ROAD ON YOUR LEFT. **PARKING:** PATRONS MAY LEAVE THEIR CARS IN THE PUB CAR
PARK WHILE THEY WALK – BUT PLEASE ASK FIRST.

This is a beautiful walk in the Blackmoor Vale. From Hinton St Mary, a charming village built of pale gold stone, footpaths lead down to the river Stour. Our path then follows the bank of the river providing an opportunity to enjoy some of its wealth of wildlife. Tall stands of reeds and rushes provide nesting sites for sedge warblers and reed buntings. Kingfishers breed in holes in the banks, herons stand motionless in the shallows, and, if you are lucky, you may even see otters. Our path leads to Cutt Mill, where the river tumbles and foams over a weir, before returning over the meadows to Hinton St Mary. This idyllic countryside inspired the work of Dorset's great poet, William Barnes.

The White Horse Inn

You would expect a lovely village like Hinton St Mary to have an attractive inn and when you visit the White Horse you will not be disappointed. Built of golden stone beneath a mossed stone-shingled roof this traditional village hostelry offers the warmest of welcomes to all. Families are made specially welcome. The lounge and public bars are separate and comfortably furnished. Low ceilings, deep window seats and huge old-fashioned fireplaces help to create a relaxed, homely atmosphere. There is a wide range of real ales, seasonally rotated. Friday night is 'pound-a-pint' night so that might be the day to choose for your walk! Cider is available and there is an extensive wine list. All the food is home-cooked and includes an à la carte menu and a specials board. When we called popular dishes included sizzling bangers, mash and peas, crusty rabbit pie and chicken with lemon and rosemary. Exciting Thai and Chinese meals are also sometimes available and there is a wide choice of vegetarian dishes.

A pretty garden overlooks the village. Opening times are from 11.15 am to 3 pm and 6.15 pm to 11 pm (12 noon to 3 pm and 7 pm to 11 pm on Sundays). Meals are served from 12 noon to 2 pm and 6.15 pm to 9 pm (7 pm to 9 pm on Sundays). Telephone: 01258 472723.

The Walk

① Take the no-through-road opposite the front porch of the pub towards the church. The tower is late 15th century and inside there is a 17th century monument to Thomas Freke who built the manor house. If you

leave the south porch of the church and bear left to the corner of the graveyard you will have a fine view of the manor. It is built on the site of a medieval abbey and the tithe barn and stables remain from those times.

Retrace your steps, turn left and walk down to the main road, the B3092.

② Cross the road and continue down the narrow lane ahead, Wood Lane. When the lane curves right, turn left following the footpath sign for Sturminster Newton. The track runs between hedges then beside the trees of Twinwood Coppice on the left and fields on the right for about ½ mile.

③ The path bears left through a narrow band of woodland to lead over a stile into a meadow. Keep ahead over the meadow for about 150 yards and look carefully for a small wooden bridge down the slope on the right. The path to it is not clear but it runs past a post supporting power cables.

④ Bear right to cross the bridge to the path beside the Stour which is on your left. Follow the riverside path over stiles and bridges past the point where the little river

71

Cutt Mill beside the river Stour

Divelish flows into the Stour. In summer the still water close to the banks is carpeted with yellow waterlilies, the 'clote' of William Barnes' poetry. Our path keeps to the riverside as it curves right then winds along the hillside following marked poles to climb past a cottage to a lane.

⑤ Turn left to see Cutt Mill in its beautiful setting. Then retrace your steps up the lane. Pass your earlier footpath on the right.

⑥ Turn right following the bridleway sign for Wood Lane. Go through a gate and walk up to a grassy crosstrack. Turn right and continue with young trees on your left and a mature wood on your right.

⑦ Navigate carefully here! When the obvious wide track curves left a little uphill keep straight on along a very narrow path through an opening in a hedge to a field. Bear right then left round the field to go through a gate. Keep ahead along the foot of a meadow, trees on your right, to a crossing track.

⑧ Turn left (you may have to unhook a wire). The track climbs to a gate on the right.

⑨ Bear right through the gate and follow the field edge, hedge on the left, to Wood Lane. Turn left and retrace your steps to the White Horse.

PLACES OF INTEREST NEARBY
Beside the White Horse is Hinton St Mary's **Millennium Garden**. A board gives details of a Roman mosaic discovered in the village in 1963.

Sturminster Newton working water mill is open from Easter to the end of September, Saturday, Sunday, Monday and Thursday, 11 am to 5 pm. Telephone: 01258 473760.

Iwerne Courtney

SPECTACULAR VIEWS FROM HAMBLEDON HILL

The Cricketers

MAP: OS EXPLORER 118 (GR 860125)   **WALK 23**   **DISTANCE:** 2½ MILES

DIRECTIONS TO START: IWERNE COURTNEY (ALSO CALLED SHROTON) LIES JUST WEST OF THE A350 BLANDFORD FORUM-SHAFTESBURY ROAD, ABOUT 5 MILES NORTH OF BLANDFORD FORUM. HEADING NORTH TURN LEFT FOR IWERNE COURTNEY AND FOLLOW THE ROAD ROUND AS IT BENDS RIGHT TO THE CHURCH ON YOUR LEFT AND A LARGE PARKING AREA ON YOUR RIGHT. **PARKING:** USE THIS AREA AS PARKING AT THE CRICKETERS IS LIMITED.

This short stroll is proof that you do not need to walk far to enjoy some of the finest scenery this lovely county has to offer! An easy climb from Iwerne Courtney brings you to the top of Hambledon Hill, an outlying spur of chalk downland crowned with the embankments of a great Iron Age fort. From this vantage point there are spectacular views west over the Blackmoor Vale, east over the Iwerne valley and the slopes of Cranborne Chase, and south over the coast to the Isle of Wight. We follow the Wessex Ridgeway with views of Hod Hill, also ringed by the embankments of an Iron Age fort, before we return along the valley to our starting point near the Cricketers pub.

The Cricketers

The Cricketers is situated in the shadow of Hambledon Hill in the heart of one of Dorset's prettiest villages. As its name suggests it is close to the village's beautifully maintained cricket pitch and the cricketing theme is very much in evidence inside with bats, balls, stumps and sketches decorating the bar and the walls – even the front door! Spacious alcoves contribute to the pub's restful and relaxed atmosphere. There is a separate restaurant. The owner takes great pride in caring properly for his customers and you can count on excellent food. The menu offers a wide choice of dishes including home-made pâtés and soups. When we called 'specials' included home-made crab cakes with lobster sauce, Lancashire hot pot and grilled pork chops with apple sauce. Fresh fish is delivered each day straight from the boats. Real ales are Spitfire (from a Kent brewery), Bass, Greene King IPA, Abbot Ale and a guest. The extensive wine list offers some interesting speciality wines.

Opening times are from 11.30 am to 2.20 pm (3 pm at weekends) and 6.30 pm to 11.30 pm. Food is served at lunchtime from 12 noon to 2 pm during the week, until 2.30 pm at weekends. In summer food is available in the evening from 6.30 pm to 9 pm; in winter from 7 pm to 9 pm. The pub is popular so if you plan a group visit let the owner know beforehand so that everything can be ready for you. Telephone: 01258 860421.

The Walk

① With the parking area on your right and the church on your left walk up the

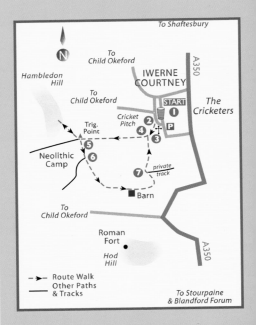

village street for a few yards then turn left along Fairfield Road passing a massive thatched barn on your left. The road curves right towards the cricket pavilion. Just before the pavilion you will see a stile and bridleway sign on the left.

② Cross the stile and, leaving the cricket pitch on your right, walk half-left diagonally up the hill towards a stone wall.

③ Go through a metal gate.

④ A few yards further on, turn right and walk up the side of a field to go through another metal gate. Continue uphill. The track leads up to a trig point on the crest of the ridge. The world of the Blackmoor Vale is spread at your feet.

⑤ Our way is left at the trig point. But first you might like to turn right to the embankments of Hambledon Hill Iron

Iwerne Courtney from the path to Hambledon Hill

Age fort. You will be rewarded by more splendid views and a wealth of wild flowers in season. Retrace your steps to the trig point and keep straight on along the ridge between fences, passing the top of our earlier path on the left. Ahead rise the ramparts of the Iron Age fort on Hod Hill. The track descends and curves right through a gate. The humps and bumps in the field on your right are the grass-covered remains of a Neolithic camp dating back to around 2,790 years BC.

⑥ Leave the Wessex Ridgeway here. From the gate the path bears left for a few yards then right to run along the foot of a hill with a wood on the left. (Ignore the parallel track closer to the wood.) Follow the path through gates until you come to a large iron barn. Keep to the path leading steeply downhill to a small wooden gate on the left. Turn left through the gate and follow the narrow path ahead through another gate and continue along the hillside, passing a wood and 'Private Track' sign on your right.

⑦ The track becomes a wide way dipping and rising along the foot of a field to bring you back to the metal gate at point 3. Bear left to retrace your steps past the cricket pitch. Turn right over the stile to follow Fairfield Road back to the High Street. Turn left to walk the few yards to the Cricketers or right to return to your car.

PLACES OF INTEREST NEARBY

Hod Hill (NT) – a well-preserved Roman fort within Iron Age embankments – is a site of rare plants and butterflies. Best approached on foot from Stourpaine.

Morden

DORSET IN MINIATURE

The Cock and Bottle

MAP: OS EXPLORER 118 (GR 913947) | **WALK 24** | **DISTANCE:** 2 OR 3¾ MILES

DIRECTIONS TO START: MORDEN LIES BESIDE THE B3075 WHICH LINKS THE A31 WITH THE A35. TURN OFF THE A31 BY THE WORLD'S END PUB AND CONTINUE FOR ABOUT 3 MILES TO THE COCK AND BOTTLE PUB ON YOUR RIGHT. FROM THE A35, FOLLOW SIGN FOR MORDEN. **PARKING:** IN THE COCK AND BOTTLE CAR PARK; IF FULL, USE THE LAYBY.

Only 6 miles or so west of Poole you will find Morden, a tiny brick, cob and thatch village set in enchanting countryside between the watermeadows of the Stour valley and the heathland north of Wareham. It is a miniature landscape of little hills and gentle valleys with small farms tucked in their hollows. We follow quiet lanes and woodland paths to East Morden, a tiny village perched on a hilltop. The shorter route then crosses Cockett Hill and follows Goodwin's Lane to return to the pub. The longer walk takes you through the woods and meadows of an old deer park with splendid views towards the coastal hills before taking the same route down Goodwin's Lane.

The Cock and Bottle

This traditional country hostlery dates back 400 years and was once a typical thatched Dorset longhouse with the family living at one end and their animals at the other! Today it is a comfortable and spacious inn with secluded alcoves ideal for family meals, two restaurants (one non-smoking) and cosy bars with open log fires on cold days. Real ales are Hall and Woodhouse's Badger Best and Tanglefoot. There are excellent house wines and an extensive wine list. Meals to suit every taste feature on the menu. When we called home-cooked dishes included spring lamb casserole in an orange sauce, steak and kidney suet pudding made to the pub's own recipe and whole local plaice served with parsley butter.

Opening times are 11 am to 3 pm and 6 pm to 11 pm. Sunday evening hours are 7 pm to 10.30 pm. Meals are served from 12 noon to 2 pm and 6 pm to 9 pm (7 pm to 9 pm on Sundays). Telephone: 01929 459238.

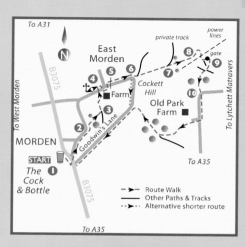

The Walk

① Leave the front door of the pub, turn right for a few yards then take the lane on the left, signed for East Morden. Continue past a lane on the left.

② When the lane curves sharply left keep straight on along a wide track. After passing a house keep ahead along a narrow path to a crosspath.

③ Turn left over a stile and bear half-right down the field towards East Morden on the opposite hillside. Cross the stile at the foot of the field and follow the grassy path ahead. Just after an attractive thatched cottage bear right then left to climb up to a T-junction in the village. Our way is right here but you might like to make a short detour and turn left to the church. Inside, a remarkable monument dated 1597 shows Thomas Erle of nearby Charborough House kneeling in prayer clad in armour. The Erles held the manor 'by service of pouring water on the King's hands on Easter or Christmas day'.

④ Return to the T-junction and follow the lane past a turning to a farm on the right and shortly after take the lane on the right.

⑤ Continue for about ¼ mile until the lane curves right.

For the shorter route follow the lane round to the right over Cockett Hill and keep to the lane as it curves right again – this is Goodwin's Lane – to bring you to the B3075. Turn right to the pub.

⑥ For the longer walk leave the lane on the first right curve and bear left. Navigate carefully here! Ignore the wide path leading

East Morden neatly arranged on a hillside

uphill and take the first narrow path leading through the woods on your right with a fence on your right. Cross a stile and keep ahead beside a field and then along a good track leading to a wood.

⑦ When the track begins to curve left look carefully for a narrow plank bridge on your right. Leave the track, turn right over the bridge, and follow the woodland path over a crosstrack with the edge of the wood on your left.

⑧ The path turns left with a fence on the left to the foot of a field. Look carefully for a track on your right and turn right up this to a gravel crosstrack. Bear left under the power lines and continue until the path swings left to a gate. Two footpaths are indicated on the right.

⑨ Turn right along the path nearest to the gate and continue along the edge of a wood with a fence on the left and go over a stile to reach crosspaths. Turn right, still along the edge of the wood. The path becomes a deep sunken way leading to the corner of a lane.

⑩ Turn right along the lane past Old Park Farm and turn right along the lane signed for Morden. After about 60 yards turn right down a narrow fenced footpath leading downhill and through woods past a joining track on the left. The path curves left to meet Goodwin's Lane. Follow the lane downhill to meet the B3075. Turn right to the pub.

PLACES OF INTEREST NEARBY
Bournemouth and **Poole** are within easy reach.

Church Knowle

THE MAGIC OF THE PURBECK HILLS
The New Inn

MAP: OS OUTDOOR LEISURE 15 (GR 938818)   **WALK 25**   **DISTANCE:** 1¾ MILES

DIRECTIONS TO START: CHURCH KNOWLE IS ABOUT 6 MILES SOUTH OF WAREHAM. TAKE THE A351, WAREHAM-SWANAGE ROAD. TURN RIGHT FOR CHURCH KNOWLE BELOW CORFE CASTLE. CONTINUE FOR ABOUT 2 MILES PAST THE CHURCH TO THE NEW INN ON YOUR LEFT. **PARKING:** IN THE NEW INN CAR PARK. HAVE A WORD WITH THE MANAGEMENT BEFORE LEAVING YOUR CAR WHILE YOU WALK.

You will enjoy some of the county's finest scenery as you follow the route of this short walk on the Isle of Purbeck. Although not strictly an island – its western boundary is only a small stream – Purbeck has a charm and character all its own. To the north lies a vast area of heathland bordering Poole Harbour and to the south great limestone cliffs confront the sea. Between the two runs a high ridge of chalk downland giving splendid views. From Church Knowle, an attractive village built of dove-grey Purbeck stone, our walk makes a gradual and fairly easy ascent to the top of the ridge and follows the crest for almost a mile. In addition to the views, this chalk downland is famous for its wild flowers and butterflies. We return to the village along the foot of the hill.

The New Inn

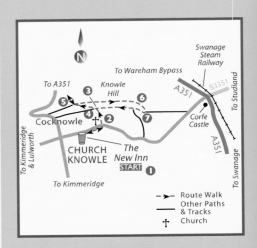

This is a delightful 16th century stone and thatch inn with panoramic views over the Purbeck Hills. It has welcomed travellers and locals alike for over 200 years. The public bar is cool and spacious, open to the rafters with plenty of room for families. A magnificent Purbeck stone fireplace dominates one wall. A cosy beamed lounge bar and non-smoking dining room provide alternative accommodation. The inn specialises in home-cooked English food with traditional roasts. When we called both lamb and pork roasts were on the wide-ranging menu as well as a delicious New Forest Game pie. And if you enjoy fish you are in for a treat, with such dishes as black bream and sea bass and fresh salmon steak served in a lobster cream and brandy sauce. The inn is also well known for its very special Blue Vinny soup.

Real ales are Flowers, Old Speckled Hen and 6X. Ciders are Strongbow and Woodpecker and there is an extensive list of well-chosen wines. The pretty garden is enclosed and gives more lovely valley views. Opening times during the week are from 11.30 am to 3 pm and 5.30 pm to 11 pm; Sundays 12 noon to 3 pm and 5.30 pm to 11 pm. Meals are served from 12 noon to 2.15 pm and 6 pm to 9.15 pm. Dogs are welcome on leads in the garden. Telephone: 01929 480357.

The Walk

① Leave the front porch of the New Inn on your right and follow the raised footpath beside the road. The footpath descends then continues through the village past Church Farm to the church of St Peter. The church dates from the 13th century and has an attractive triple chancel arch and a fine altar tomb retaining all its brasses. This was ordered for John Clavell who died in 1609. It shows him as 'husband of these two wives'. Pictured on either side of him are Myllicent, who died in 1571, and Susan, who died in 1618.

② Pass the church on your left and turn left following the sign for Knowle Hill. Keep straight on with the church wall close on your left. Go through a gate and follow the grassy path ahead towards the foot of Knowle Hill. Cross the stile by a gate to a crossing path and footpath signs.

③ Turn left following the sign for Cocknowle. Continue for only about 30 yards.

④ At this point the path divides. Take the right-hand narrow path which climbs gradually uphill through the gorse and scrub. This is home for many birds including yellowhammers, linnets and nightingales. Cross a stile and continue

Looking south from Church Knowle hill

phill. As you near the top the scrub gives way to downland grasses and the path is indistinct. Keep straight ahead over the grass to the ridgeway crossing path.

(5) Our way is right here, but first cross the ridgeway path and continue for just a few yards to enjoy a magnificent view north over the heath and Poole Harbour. Retrace your steps to the ridgeway path. Follow the brow of the hill to go through a gate and continue with a fence on your right. Cross the next stile and keep ahead past Bronze Age burial mounds on your left. As early as 1800 BC Bronze Age people came this way. A wealthy society developed trading in salt, bronze, Baltic amber, Irish gold and Whitby jet. Grave goods included finely worked bronze and gold daggers and bracelets and necklaces of blue faience beads from Egypt.

(6) When you come to a stone marked 'No Path Ahead' bear right following the wide terraced path down the hillside. In summer the turf is starred with yellow horseshoe vetch, food for the caterpillars of the rare Adonis Blue butterfly, recognisable by its bright sky blue wings.

(7) At the foot of the hill you meet a crossing track. Turn right to follow this to rejoin our former route at point 3. Bear left to retrace your steps to the New Inn.

PLACES OF INTEREST NEARBY

Corfe Castle, imposing ruins commanding a gap in the downs. Open 10 am to 5.30 pm from March to October and 11 am to 3.30 pm from November to February. Telephone: 01929 481294.

Swanage Steam Railway runs to Corfe Castle. Telephone: 01929 424276 (timetable); 01929 425800 (bookings).

Sturminster Marshall

WALKING IN THE STOUR VALLEY

The Red Lion Inn

MAP: OS EXPLORER 118 (GR 951004) | **WALK 26** | **DISTANCE:** 2¾ MILES

DIRECTIONS TO START: STURMINSTER MARSHALL LIES EAST OF THE A350 BETWEEN BLANDFORD FORUM AND POOLE. LEAVE THE A350 SIGNED FOR THE VILLAGE CENTRE. THE RED LION IS OPPOSITE THE CHURCH ON YOUR RIGHT. **PARKING:** IN THE RED LION INN CAR PARK.

The rich watermeadows of the Stour valley are the main feature of this walk but there is much more to enjoy. Sturminster Marshall is a spacious village with many attractive houses set around three greens. In the oldest part narrow lanes cluster around a green with a maypole and close by a second green retains the village stocks. Our way crosses the meadows to White Mill Bridge, reputed to be the oldest and most beautiful bridge in Dorset. It takes its name from the nearby corn mill which stands on a site of a mill mentioned in the Domesday Book. If you wish you could make a short detour beside the river before returning to our starting point, the Red Lion Inn.

The Red Lion Inn

The Red Lion is situated in a tranquil corner of the village, not far from the Stour, and it is hard to believe that a busy main road is only a few minutes away. This traditional village inn has offered a warm welcome, rest and refreshment to travellers for many centuries as it stands beside the old road leading east from Dorchester to Wimborne. A building 'at the sign of the Red Lion' is recorded in the deeds in 1706. Could one of these travellers be still with us? I was told that a mysterious presence can be felt near the walled-in fireplace of the bar! We could well understand a reluctance to leave. The comfortable wood-panelled bar offers well-kept real ales including Tanglefoot and Dorset Best, Dry Blackthorn or draught cider and a choice of excellent wines. There is a separate non-smoking restaurant. The menu both in the bar and restaurant is interesting and varied. Specials are listed each day and all the food is home-made. Starters when we called included 'Moorish Salad' – a mouthwatering dish of prawns and apricots soaked in white wine – and chicken liver pâté in port wine. Among the main meals were steak and stout pie, 'Mississippi Roadrunner' – breast of chicken with Cajun spices and melon – and 'Out of Africa', roasted haunch of Springbok. There is a tempting fish menu as well as vegetarian alternatives and a children's menu.

Opening times from Monday to Saturday are 11 am to 2.30 pm and 7 pm to 11 pm, with the usual Sunday times. Food is served from 12 noon to 2 pm and 7 pm to 9.30 pm. The gardens are pleasantly quiet and secluded. Telephone: 01258 857319.

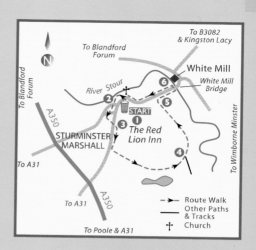

The Walk

NB: Wear wellies or strong shoes after prolonged rain.

① Cross the road in front of the pub and go through the gate into the churchyard. After a few yards turn left along a grassy path leaving the church on your right. Turn left by the churchyard wall to a wooden walkway leading down to meadows by the Stour. Go through a gate and walk along the embankment of the flood defences with the river on your right for about 200 yards. Then bear half-left diagonally across the meadow to go through a gate to a lane.

② Turn right and continue for about 50 yards then turn left along a footpath to emerge in front of Maypole Green. There has probably been a maypole here since the first fair was held in 1101. Turn right leaving the maypole on your left to meet a road. Continue past another green and take the first road on your left, opposite a private road, to the High Street.

③ Turn right down the High Street as far

The medieval White Mill Bridge crosses the Stour near Sturminster Marshall

as Moor Lane (signed for the golf course). Turn left along Moor Lane which becomes a leafy track winding past the golf course on the left and meadows on the right. Keep to the main track as it curves left past gravel pits, now lakes and a haven for wildlife.

④ At the crossing track bear left to a road.

⑤ Turn right beside the road to White Mill Bridge. A bridge on this site has been recorded since 1174. It is built in Norman style with eight arches resting on 800 year old oak piles. The arches are attractively ribbed with alternate layers of white limestone and red sandstone. A plaque warns that anyone caught damaging the structure will be transported! Beyond the bridge, medieval White Mill has been restored by the National Trust. It is open for guided tours between Easter and October at weekends, 12 noon to 5 pm.

⑥ Retrace your steps to the bridge. If you would like a stroll by the water take the footpath on the left leading to the river bank. Then retrace your steps, cross the bridge and follow the lane for a little under ¹⁄₂ mile past the curved cob walls of rows of thatched cottages to return to the Red Lion.

PLACES OF INTEREST NEARBY

Badbury Rings, off the B3082 to the north – a splendid Iron Age hill fort and an important centre in Roman Britain at the meeting place of several major roads.

Kingston Lacy (NT) – a magnificent mansion with a richly decorated interior and fine paintings. Open April to October, 12 noon to 5.30 pm; closed Thursday and Friday. Telephone: 01202 882493.

Wimborne Minster – enchanting market town. For details ring the Tourist Office: 01202 886116.

Tarrant Monkton

IN THE VALLEY OF THE 'TRESPASSING' STREAM

The Langton Arms

MAP: OS EXPLORER 118 (GR 944089)	**WALK 27**	**DISTANCE:** 3 MILES

DIRECTIONS TO START: TARRANT MONKTON IS BEST APPROACHED VIA THE A354 BLANDFORD FORUM-SALISBURY ROAD. TURN FOR THE VILLAGE IN TARRANT HINTON, CONTINUE THROUGH TARRANT LAUNCESTON AND AFTER ABOUT ¼ MILE AS YOU ENTER TARRANT MONKTON TURN RIGHT OVER THE FORD AND FOLLOW THE ROAD ROUND TO THE LANGTON ARMS. TO AVOID THE FORD, KEEP STRAIGHT ON AND TAKE THE NEXT TURNING ON THE RIGHT TO THE PUB. **PARKING:** AT THE FRONT OR SIDE OF THE PUB.

Glimpsed from the main road the Tarrant valley appears a mere ripple in an open landscape but if you turn aside and follow the little chalk stream as it flows south carving a secret valley in the downs you will discover a succession of enchanting villages. Tarrant Monkton, mostly cob and thatch surrounded by lush streamside meadows, is one of the most charming. The church stands prominently on the hillside above the river. The square tower was built early in the 13th century. Inside you will find a wheel dating from 1610, once used to swing the tenor bell, a Norman font and a finely-carved 18th century pulpit. Close to the church is our starting point, the Langton Arms.

The Langton Arms

Dark-thatched and built of warm red brick, the Langton Arms is a most attractive inn. The oldest part of the pub dates from the 17th century and inside the bar area you will find the rich wood panelling and heavily-beamed ceilings typical of that time. This friendly pub with its skittle alley – Dorset folk are great skittlers – is the centre of the community and there is a warm family atmosphere. The restaurant is housed in a beautifully converted former stable. And you can rely on finding excellent food. The pub is a free house run by a local farming family and everything is home-cooked and, whenever possible, obtained from local sources. Among the most popular dishes are traditionally made faggots, pot-roasted wild rabbit and game pie cooked in red wine and redcurrant gravy. Examples of lighter meals are king prawns wrapped in crisp filo pastry and a delicious country farmhouse pâté, followed by desserts such as meringues sandwiched with fresh cream and a good old-fashioned favourite, bread-and-butter pudding. Five real ales are on tap including Ringwood Best and four guests.

The pub is open from 11 am to 11 pm during the week with the usual Sunday opening hours. Meals are served from 12 noon to 2.30 pm and 6 pm to 9.30 pm. The Stables Restaurant is open in the evenings from Wednesday to Saturday and at lunchtime on Sundays. For a longer stay the pub offers six guest rooms built around an attractive courtyard. Telephone: 01258 830225.

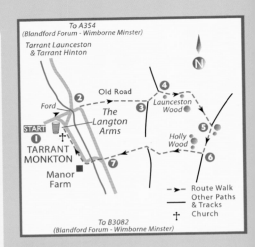

The Walk

① With the front entrance to the pub on your left walk down the lane past the war memorial on your left and a phone box on your right. Continue past thatched cottages with brilliantly colourful gardens and cross the packhorse bridge over the Tarrant. The ford is on your left. This was the main route from London to Weymouth until the Great Western Turnpike (the present A354) was constructed through Tarrant Hinton in 1755 and many coaches must have splashed through the river at this point!

② Keep ahead up the lane following the sign for Spetisbury. When the road curves right leave it and walk straight ahead up the old road. The narrow asphalt track becomes a pleasant grass-and-gravel terraced way climbing gently up the side of the valley. As you gain height there are splendid views over Cranborne Chase. After about ³/₄ mile you reach a metal barrier and a crosstrack.

③ Turn left. The track bears a little right to another crosstrack in front of Launceston Wood.

Bluebells in Holly Wood near Tarrant Monkton

came this way a young roe broke cover and bounded gracefully across our path!

⑥ Look for the blue arrow bridleway sign marking a track on the right and turn right towards Holly Wood. Continue along the track with the wood on your right – a marvellous sight in spring when carpeted with bluebells – and when the wood ends step over a log and keep straight ahead across a field. Go through a gate, turn right for a few yards to pass a barrier then turn left to follow the grassy track down the hillside into the Tarrant valley.

⑦ At the road, turn right for a few yards then bear left along the lane signed for Tarrant Monkton. The lane leads over the Tarrant before curving right in front of Manor Farm to bring you back to the Langton Arms.

④ Bear right with the wood on your right and follow the path past tracks to right and left. Trees give way to open country and our track veers right to meet crosspaths.

⑤ Turn right to walk beside a wood on your left. Keep an eye out for deer. As we

PLACES OF INTEREST NEARBY

The **Royal Signals Museum** at Blandford Camp, just west of Tarrant Monkton, tells the history of military communications since the Crimean War. Displays include vehicles and interactive exhibits. Open all year Monday to Friday, 10 am to 5 pm. From June to September it is open at weekends too, 10 am to 4 pm. Telephone: 01258 482248.

Sixpenny Handley

A DOWNLAND RAMBLE IN CRANBORNE CHASE

The Roebuck Inn

MAP: OS EXPLORER 118 (GR 998172)   **WALK 28**   **DISTANCE:** 3 MILES

DIRECTIONS TO START: SIXPENNY HANDLEY IS 8 MILES NORTH-WEST OF CRANBORNE
BESIDE THE B3081 SHAFTESBURY-RINGWOOD ROAD. TURN FOR THE VILLAGE OFF
THE A354 BLANDFORD-SALISBURY ROAD. THE ROEBUCK FACES THE HIGH STREET.
PARKING: IN THE PUB CAR PARK.

Many Dorset villages have fascinating names but one of the most intriguing must be Sixpenny Handley. Somehow the Saxon words for a hill top (*seax pena*) became Sixpenny and those for a high clearing (*hean leagh*) became Handley. In the 13th century the two Saxon settlements were united and together they staunchly resisted decimalisation in 1971! It is an interesting rather than a conventionally pretty village but Sixpenny Handley has pleasant shops, a school, a Norman church and, of course, a friendly pub. From the pub we follow footpaths and lanes to explore some of this delightful countryside and discover Deanland, an attractive village tucked away in a remote valley.

The Roebuck Inn

The Roebuck is a warm-hearted village pub. It is deservedly popular and though busy when we called, we received a smiling welcome and found comfortable seats in one of the spacious bar areas which, like the restaurant, is furnished with solid oak tables and chairs specially imported from Holland. And the Roebuck is a perfect pub for walkers with hearty appetites! All the food is home-made and includes an all-day 'Mega Breakfast' – two rashers of bacon, two sausages, tomatoes, mushrooms, fried eggs and hash browns. Another popular dish is a delicious savoury bacon and cheese melt served on garlic bread. Examples of other dishes on the menu are peppered steak in a brandy and cream sauce and chicken served in white wine. If you happen to call on a Friday evening around 10 o'clock you can enjoy a free supper! Families are welcome and children have their own menu.

Real ales are Ringwood Best, True Glory, Fortyniner and Old Thumper. In summer other ales include the enchantingly named 'Boondoggle', Summer Lightning and Thunderstorm. Ciders and a choice of wines are also available. The inn offers accommodation and there is a large sunny garden.

Opening times during the week are 11.30 am to 3 pm and 6.30 pm to 11 pm. On Saturdays the Roebuck is open all day and on Sundays 12 noon to 3 pm and 7 pm to 10.30 pm. Meals are served 12 noon to 2.30 pm and 7 pm to 9.30 pm except on Monday evenings. Telephone: 01725 552002.

The Walk

① Leave the front door of the pub and turn right. Now turn immediately right again down a narrow lane past the post office on the left. Keep ahead down a narrow hedged path and go over a stile to a crosspath.

② Turn left to walk beside a field with a hedge on your left. Disregard a stile and footpath sign on the left and keep straight on to pass another footpath sign on the left. Continue between some wooden posts.

③ Bear half-right diagonally, following a grassy path down a meadow (indicated by a red sign for the Sixpenny Handley Roundwalk). From the hillside enjoy the fine view over Deanland and the wooded slopes of Cranborne Chase to the Wiltshire downs. The path leads through a gap in a hedge and continues with a fence on your right to bring you to Dean Lane.

④ Turn left along this quiet lane to pass a bridleway on the left (our return route) and walk through Deanland village.

Will the signpost to '6D Handley' prove a mystery in the future?

⑦ Cross double stiles and turn left with a hedge still on your left. Go through a gate and keep ahead along a narrow meadow path. Cross a stile and, aiming to leave the buildings of Snowpuddle Farm (splendid name!) over on your left, bear slightly right over the next field. Go over another stile to a track.

⑧ Turn left to follow the track for about ½ mile past Hunt Corner Farm and Barber's Coppice to a wide bridleway on the left.

⑨ Leave the track and turn left down this attractive grassy way to rejoin Dean Lane.

⑩ Turn right along the lane and shortly after turn right again to retrace your steps along our outward bound route beside the fence then up the meadow. Turn left, still retracing your steps, to follow the footpath back to the village and the Roebuck Inn.

⑤ Pass a telephone box on the left and after about 60 yards turn left through an iron gate. Bear a little right to cross a stile. Turn left to walk up a field keeping a wood on your left. When the wood ceases keep straight on with a fence now on your left.

⑥ At the top of the field turn right following the footpath sign (the route differs slightly from the OS map) with a hedge on your left.

PLACES OF INTEREST NEARBY

The Larmer Tree Gardens, about 5 miles west of Sixpenny Handley, just over the Wiltshire border near Tollard Royal, are historic gardens created by General Pitt Rivers. They contain oriental-inspired buildings, a Roman temple and an open-air theatre. Tea rooms and gift shop. Open between Easter and October, 11 am to 6 pm, daily except Saturdays and festivals. Telephone: 01725 516228.

Gussage All Saints

WHERE ROMAN MET BRITON

The Drovers' Inn

MAP: OS EXPLORER 118 (GR 003107)	**WALK 29**	**DISTANCE:** 3 MILES

DIRECTIONS TO START: GUSSAGE ALL SAINTS IS ABOUT 7 MILES EAST OF BLANDFORD FORUM. TURN FOR THE VILLAGE OFF THE A354 BLANDFORD FORUM-SALISBURY ROAD. DRIVE THROUGH GUSSAGE ST MICHAEL. BEAR LEFT AS YOU ENTER GUSSAGE ALL SAINTS TO DRIVE THROUGH THE VILLAGE. THE DROVERS' INN IS SET BACK FROM THE ROAD ON YOUR LEFT. **PARKING:** PATRONS MAY LEAVE CARS IN THE PUB CAR PARK BUT PLEASE ASK FIRST.

Gussage All Saints is an old-world village of thatched whitewashed cottages beautifully situated in a downland valley. At the foot of the High Street the tiny Gussage stream runs under a series of small brick bridges. This is one of the most historic areas of Dorset crossed by Ackling Dyke, a road built by the Romans in the 1st century AD to connect the important town of Old Sarum, just north of Salisbury (now little remains except a few remnants of a Norman castle), with Badbury Rings, west of Wimborne. Our walk leaves the village along one of the wide tracks used in the past by drovers and climbs to give splendid views before we follow in the footsteps of the legions and descend Ackling Dyke to return to our starting point, the Drovers' Inn.

The Drovers' Inn

You will receive a warm welcome in this comfortable 16th century inn. The bar with its heavily-beamed ceilings supported by wooden pillars is lit by a row of small, deep-set windows and contains enormous fireplaces. After a brisk walk on a cold day you can draw up an armchair and relax in front of a blazing log fire. And if you enjoy real ales you have a real treat in store. The Drovers' offers five: Ringwood Best, Fortyniner, True Glory, Old Thumper and in summer you can sample the interestingly-named 'Boondoggle'. In winter, porter is on offer. There is also an occasional guest ale. Traditional cider is on tap and among the wines we found a local one from Ringwood. All the food is home-cooked and you can choose from eight different 'Drovers' Lunches'. You might try farmhouse pâté or one of five cheeses which include Dorset's own Blue Vinney. The menu offers a range of mouthwatering options, for example a tempting chicken, ham and leek pie.

Opening times are from 11 am to 3 pm and 6 pm to 11 pm with the usual Sunday opening times. Food is served from 12 noon to 2 pm and 7 pm to 9 pm and there is a separate restaurant.

There are two gardens overlooking the valley. The inn is deservedly popular and if you plan a group visit do let the staff know beforehand so that everything can be ready for you. If planning an early start before the pub is open it is wise to phone in advance. Telephone: 01258 840084.

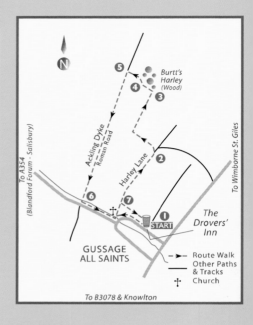

The Walk

① Leave the front porch of the Drovers' and turn right along the village street. When the road begins to curve left, turn right past the war memorial to walk up Harley Lane passing the church on the left. The asphalt shortly gives way to a grass-and-gravel track which climbs gently uphill for a little over ½ mile. The ascent is easy and soon you are rewarded by splendid views west over the Gussage valley.

② At this point the track divides. Take the left-hand path which descends diagonally down a short slope to meet a wide, hedged track. Bear left along this beautiful grassy way – a real drovers' track with plenty of room for their animals to graze – and keep to the track as it curves right and leads gradually up to a wood, Burtt's Harley.

The Drovers' road near Gussage All Saints

③ In front of the wood the track bears left with the wood close on the right.

④ When you come to the edge of the wood bear a little left to leave the trees behind and cross a stile. Continue beside a meadow with a hedge on your left. The meadow has been 'set aside' and is full of wild flowers and butterflies in summer.

⑤ The meadow path leads to a broad crosstrack, Ackling Dyke. Turn left along this historic road. It is still over 40 ft wide – carefully planned to allow ten legionaries to walk abreast. Originally it would have been raised about 6 ft above the ground

with deep ditches on either side. Time has worn it down but the embankment on the right gives some idea of its original height. It is no surprise that so many Roman roads survive today, often running beneath our modern highways. The Romans believed in building roads to last. The earth from the ditches was heaped in the centre and large heavy stones were placed on top as a foundation. This was surfaced with a rammed layer of fine aggregate made from the best locally available material. For Ackling Dyke the Romans used flint beach pebbles brought from nearby Pentridge Hill. Follow Ackling Dyke past a barrier to the road.

⑥ Turn left beside the road to walk into Gussage All Saints. Follow the road as it curves left over the Gussage stream. When the road turns right keep straight on to retrace your steps up Harley Lane past the church.

⑦ After a few yards turn right into the entrance to College Farm. Continue past the farm buildings and take the narrow footpath ahead to cross a stile. Follow the field path with a hedge on your left to cross another lane to a track. Turn right to the Drovers' Inn.

PLACES OF INTEREST NEARBY
Knowlton Circles, just to the east of Gussage All Saints – a mysterious ruined church in the middle of a circular neolithic henge monument.

Horton

OVER THE CHASE TO A FOLLY

Drusilla's Inn

MAP: OS EXPLORER 118 (GR 039074)	**WALK 30**	DISTANCE: 2½ MILES

DIRECTIONS TO START: HORTON IS 9 MILES NORTH OF WIMBORNE MINSTER. FOLLOW HORTON SIGNS FROM EITHER THE A31, POOLE-SOUTHAMPTON ROAD (TRAVELLING WEST). OR THE B3078, WIMBORNE-SALISBURY ROAD (TRAVELLING EAST). THE INN FACES THE ROAD ¼ MILE EAST OF THE VILLAGE. **PARKING:** IN THE INN CAR PARK.

Cranborne Chase was once wild and remote, a hunting ground for kings and the haunt of poachers. Although some of the area is now farmed we can still enjoy wonderful walks in this lovely countryside of rolling downland, secret valleys and ancient beech woods. Horton lies in a quiet valley on the Chase's southern fringe. From the inn, woodland paths lead to Haythorne, a picturesque cluster of mostly thatched houses around a tree-shaded green. We cross the meadows to explore Horton village before following a ridge path with splendid views and returning through Ferndown Forest.

Drusilla's Inn

The pub owes its unusual name to former owners who were German. Drusilla is a goose girl in German mythology. Dating from the 17th century, this thatched inn, its cob walls faced with rose-coloured brick, looks more like a country cottage than a pub. Inside, you will find the same cottage-like atmosphere. The bar areas are particularly attractive with heavily-beamed ceilings, huge fireplaces and pretty diamond-paned windows. The Tower Room restaurant is housed in a matching octagonal extension. The menu offers a wide choice of traditional home-cooked food. When we called, it included a mouthwatering chicken, ham and mushroom pie and an inviting savoury lasagne. Fish dishes are a speciality. From a range of bar snacks you might choose a 'double header' – a hot baguette containing succulent pork sausages topped with toasted cheese. There are vegetarian options and a children's menu. Among the sweets are Dorset apple cake and home-made profiteroles. Real ales include Ringwood Best, 6X and Fortyniner, ciders are Thatchers and Blackthorn, and wines include some from the nearby Horton Estate vineyard.

The pub is open on weekdays from 11 am to 3.30 pm and 6 pm to 11 pm, all day Saturday, and on Sunday from 12 noon to 3 pm and 6.30 pm to 9.30 pm. Meals are served from 12 noon to 2 pm and 6 pm to 9.30 pm. Telephone: 01258 840297.

The Walk

① Leave the front door of the pub and turn left past the car park. Take the

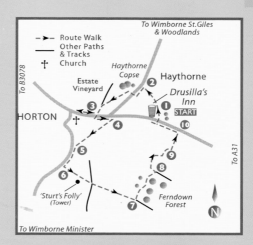

woodland footpath immediately on the left. Cross a stile to continue over paddocks with a hedge close on your left to go over another stile. Keep ahead along a narrow path with a fence on the right. The path bears left to a gravel track which runs between lawns through Haythorne. Follow the gravel track to a lane.

② Turn left beside the lane with Haythorne Copse on your right. Pass the Horton village sign and after a few yards turn right following the sign 'Footpath to Horton'. Walk through the copse, cross a stile and descend the meadow path which bears right over another stile to the track to the vineyard. Turn left to the road.

③ You might like to turn right to visit Horton village and the church of St Wolfrida. She was abbess of a Benedictine abbey – now vanished – founded here in AD 961. If so, retrace your steps to point 3 after your visit and keep straight on beside the road. Otherwise, turn left at point 3.

④ After about 200 yards, opposite a lane to Woodlands, turn right over a stile. The

Horton Tower, locally known as 'Sturt's Folly'

⑥ Bear left up the drive to go through a gate and follow a white track along the top of the ridge past the hexagonal six-storeyed brick tower known locally as 'Sturt's Folly'. It was erected by Humphrey Sturt, an 18th century landowner passionately keen on hunting. It is said he had the tower built to watch the hunt when he became too infirm to ride! The tower is now used as a transmitter for mobile phones.

Follow the ridge for about ³⁄₄ mile and go through the gate into Ferndown Forest.

⑦ After a few yards turn left along the footpath which runs just inside the forest to a crosspath.

⑧ Turn left to leave the wood and bear a little right to continue with trees close on your right beside a meadow. Cross a stile and walk up the field ahead. The path doglegs right then left, still with trees on the right.

⑨ After about 80 yards look for double stiles on the right. Cross these stiles and bear left to resume your former heading with the trees now on your left. Keep ahead over meadows and two stiles to the road.

⑩ Turn left for about 200 yards to Drusilla's Inn.

path is not clear but cross the meadow to the corner of a fence, then keep the same heading to rejoin the fence and cross a stile. Bear left with a fence on the left then leave the fence as it turns uphill and keep straight on to a footpath sign about 100 yards to the left of a barn. Cross double stiles and bear half-right over a track. Keep the same heading over the meadow to cross a stile to a lane.

⑤ Turn left up the lane for about 200 yards, then look carefully for a blue bridleway arrow on a post low down in the hedge beside an asphalt drive on your left.

PLACES OF INTEREST NEARBY
Horton Estate Vineyard is open on Saturdays, 10 am to 4 pm, and Sundays in August, for free tastings and sales.